TWAYNE'S WORLD AUTHORS SERIES

A Survey of the World's Literature

Sylvia E. Bowman, Indiana University
GENERAL EDITOR

FRANCE

Maxwell A. Smith, Guerry Professor of French, Emeritus
The University of Chattanooga
Former Visiting Professor in Modern Languages
The Florida State University

EDITOR

Gérard de Nerval

TWAS 326

Gérard de Nerval

Gérard de Nerval

By ROBERT EMMET JONES

Massachusetts Institute of Technology

Twayne Publishers, Inc.   ::   New York

Library of Congress Cataloging in Publication Data

Jones, Robert Emmet, 1928–
  Gérard de Nerval.

  (Twayne's world authors series, TWAS 326. France)
  Bibliography: p. 181
  1. Gérard de Nerval, Gérard Labrunie, known as,
1808–1855.
PQ2260.G36Z66   848'.7'09   74-4085
ISBN 0-8057-2652-7

This book is dedicated to

Thelma Richman
Otis Fellows
William Bottiglia

with appreciation and thanks

Contents

About the Author

Robert Emmet Jones, now Professor of French and the Humanities at the Massachusetts Institute of Technology, has also taught at the University of Georgia, the University of Pennsylvania, and Columbia University where he earned his doctoral degree. Professor Jones's special fields of study are French poetry of the nineteenth century, European and American drama of the twentieth century, and theories of literary criticism.

Professor Jones has published *The Alienated Hero in Modern French Drama* and *Panorama de la nouvelle critique en France*, as well as a number of articles on such authors as Rimbaud, Tennessee Williams, Lenormand, and Camus in professional journals in the United States and Europe. He is currently studying the relationship between major French plays, the opera libretti derived from them, and the music to which they have been set in order to define the function of drama in the world of opera.

Preface

The aim of this book is to acquaint the general reader with the works of Gérard de Nerval. Although I have tried to deal as little as possible with biographical material, I feel that since many of the poet's works, and especially his greatest ones, are to a large extent dependent on a knowledge of it, I must present certain details of his life without which his works cannot be fully appreciated. Of all the writers of this epoch Nerval is the most difficult for the modern reader, even though he is perhaps the most contemporary of the Romantics in subject and style. Nerval created and lived in a private world that is accessible, though with some difficulty, through his writings. The fact that he experienced several sieges of madness and of these created, either as therapy or from creative necessity, many of his major pieces of literature necessitates a knowledge of both his personal and literary obsessions, for of them he created remarkable artistic documents.

Because of the esoteric, hermetic, and mystic aspects of his work, Nerval is difficult to study without the use of innumerable references to explain to the reader what he is saying. However, I have tried to present his works with as few footnotes as possible, for they *can* be enjoyed as works of literature even when everything is not explained. Many of his writings have been examined in detail. Some, including several poems, are of minor artistic value, but I have tried to show his development as a poet, and these works are often good illustrations of that development. Some works, a few perhaps of major importance, have been treated cursorily or, as with his attempts at long fiction or the theatre, completely ignored because he added nothing to the development of those genres. Nerval is important today because he wrote poems and prose works that are unique in French literature, and it is to these pieces that I have turned my attention. While it is relatively simple to demonstrate Nerval's development from a minor poet to a major one, it is less easy to show the process of his becoming a great prose writer because his major prose works were all published within the space of four years and they differ markedly from the published fragments that he had composed earlier in his career. I have therefore tried to examine individual works and discover why they are, or miss being, masterpieces. Instead of studying the *oeuvre* as a whole, I have concentrated, even though they may be artistic failures, on the pieces that are of interest today and, hopefully, of permanent interest.

Nerval was an erratic artist, but he was a great one. His work is a fine example of the process of artistic creation and indicates what lies beneath and behind the work of art. Unlike most of the other Romantic writers, he created his own private world of obsessions, dreams, and memories, and it is this universe that will be studied in this book. Unfortunately, no critical study of his works exists in English. I hope this book will fill the lacuna.

ROBERT EMMET JONES

Boston, Massachusetts

Chronology

1808   Gérard Labrunie, who later calls himself Gérard de Nerval, is born in Paris on May 22.

1810   Death of Nerval's mother in Silesia on November 29. Nerval goes to live with his great-uncle, Antoine Boucher, at Mortefontaine.

1814   Return of Dr. Labrunie, Gérard's father, from the Napoleonic wars.

1820   Nerval enters the Collège Charlemagne where he meets Théophile Gautier.

1820   On May 30 death of Antoine Boucher with whom Nerval spent his vacations from 1814 to 1820.

1826   Publication of *Elégies nationales*, his first work.

1826–   Translation of Goethe's *Faust*.
1827

1828   Publication of the translation of *Faust*. Nerval meets Victor Hugo.

1828   Death of Nerval's grandmother on August 8.

1829   *Huit scènes de Faust*, music by Hector Berlioz.

1830   Publication of *Choix des poésies de Ronsard* and translations of *Poésies allemandes*.

1830   Nerval attends the première of *Hernani* on February 25.

1832–   Medical student in Paris.
1834

1834   Death of Nerval's grandfather on January 19. Nerval inherits 30,000 francs. Travels to the Midi and Italy later in the year.

1835   Moves to the Impasse du Doyenné. Period of *La Bohème galante*.

1835   Founds the review *Le Monde dramatique* in May.

1836   Liquidation of *Le Monde dramatique*. Nerval is bankrupt.

1837   Première of *Piquillo* on October 31, Nerval's first produced dramatic work, with Jenny Colon of whom he is enamored.

1838   Marriage of Jenny Colon to Louis-Gabriel Leplus on April 11. Trip to Germany with Alexandre Dumas in August.

1839   *L'Alchimiste* (written with Dumas) at the Théâtre de la Renaissance on April 10. *Léo Burckart* at the Porte-Saint-Martin on April 16.

1839– Trip to Vienna. Back in Paris in March, 1840.
1840
1840   Translation of the *Second Faust*. In October, trip to Belgium. Meets Jenny Colon and Marie Pleyel in Brussels on December 15. Death of Sophie Dawes, baronne Adrien de Feuchères.
1841   First attack of madness on February 21 or 23. At Dr. Esprit Blanche's clinic in Montmartre from March 21–November 21.
1842   Death of Jenny Colon on June 5. In December, trip to the Middle East.
1843   Return from the Middle East in December.
1844   Completes documentation for *Voyage en Orient*.
1848   Translations of Heine in July.
1849   *Les Monténégrins* produced at the Opéra-Comique on March 31. Another brief attack of madness in April.
1850   *Le Chariot d'enfant* at the Odéon on May 13. Treated for nervous depression in June.
1851   Publication of *Voyage en Orient*.
1851   Another attack of mental illness in September. Treated by Dr. Emile Blanche at Passy. *L'Imagier de Harlem* at the Porte-Saint-Martin on December 27.
1852   *Les Illuminés* in November.
1853   *Petits Châteaux de Bohème* and *Contes et Facéties* published. Serious mental attack on August 25. Again at Dr. Blanche's at Passy, where he remains until May 27, 1854. Publication of "El Desdichado" in an article by Dumas in *Le Mousquetaire* on December 10.
1854   Trip to Germany on May 27. Another relapse. *Les Filles du feu* and *Les Chimères*. Back at Dr. Blanche's in August. *Aurélia*.
1855   Nerval is found hanged from a lamp post on the Rue de la Vieille-Lanterne on January 26.

CHAPTER 1

Outer Worlds and Inner Worlds

GÉRARD de Nerval (1808–1855)[1] was born into a century that produced many of the greatest artists in all of French literature. The first sixty years or so of the nineteenth century, a period commonly referred to as Romantic by literary historians, gave birth to a series of masterpieces in poetry and prose that in breadth and inventiveness is unequalled in French history. From the publication in 1801 of Chateaubriand's *Atala* to the appearance of *Les Fleurs du mal* of Baudelaire in 1857, the Romantic revolution, if such it really was in the strictest sense of the term, in the fine arts, music, and literature took place. Its success had already been achieved in certain fields and it was succeeding in others by the time Nerval had reached his twentieth birthday. With the exception of Gautier, Musset, and Baudelaire, the major Romantic writers were older than Nerval; Stendhal by twenty-six years, Lamartine by eighteen, Vigny by eleven, Balzac by nine, Hugo by six, and Sainte-Beuve by four; and most of them were established or controversial literary figures when Nerval published his first work in 1826. Yet Nerval participated in many of Romanticism's triumphs and created within the movement his own particular niche, one that was quite different from those of his predecessors and contemporaries. His *growth* as an imaginative artist was rivaled in his own time only by Delacroix, Berlioz, Hugo, Balzac, and Stendhal, and, like them, he created a world that was unique.

I Romanticism[2]

Romanticism arrived late in France. The Classical tradition based on clarity, reason, and restraint had dominated the European mentality for more than a hundred years, but even in the early eighteenth century it was beginning to show signs

13

of deterioration and sterility. While Germany and England in the latter part of the eighteenth century had already broken away from the Classicism of Lessing and Pope and were developing the new approaches to art which came to be called Romanticism, the French, although somewhat aware of the movement from the books of Mme de Staël, *De la littérature* (1800) and *De l'Allemagne* (1810), remained bound by the rigid forms and rules of Classicism.

It is generally agreed that Romanticism as such began officially in France with the publication in 1820 of Lamartine's *Méditations poétiques*, and that it triumphed in 1830 when Hugo's *Hernani* succeeded at the Comédie-Française. Yet by 1832 the major Romantic writers of England and Germany were either dead (Byron, Blake, Shelley, Keats, Scott, Goethe, Schiller, Kleist, Richter, Hoffman) or had created their major works twenty or more years before (Wordsworth, Coleridge, Hölderlin). Thus French Romanticism, although it owed much to England and Germany, differed from that of the northern countries not only because it was, in broader European connotations, essentially *retardataire*, but because of the special orientation of the French mind that continued to be influenced by traditional aesthetic and rational values. Beginning as a political movement and, at the outset, conservative in its allegiances, French Romanticism differs from that of the northern countries where, when political concepts were involved, they were generally of a liberal nature. Romanticism in France is inextricably tied to the political climate of the time. The young writers were horrified by the excesses of the French Revolution of which the Empire was an outgrowth. Yet for many of them the era of Napoleon had a mystique all its own centered in the person of the Emperor. It was seen as a period when any man of goodwill and talent could succeed and perhaps become a hero, and heroism, as the young writers were to discover, was nonexistent under the Bourbons. From 1815 to about 1825, however, most of the Romantics were pleased by the return to legitimacy with the restoration of the Bourbon dynasty which hopefully would guarantee individual rights and freedom of thought and expression.[3]

The early career of Victor Hugo best illustrates the modification and evolution of Romantic political thought. Between 1819 and 1821 he wrote for *Le Conservateur littéraire*, one of the first Romantic journals in France. Influenced by Chateaubriand, he was a monarchist and supporter of the Church, and believed that Classicism should be continued but revivified. These beliefs are seen again in Hugo's preface to his *Odes et poésies diverses* (1822) in which he writes that he had two intentions in publishing his book—literary and political—but that the second was the consequence of the first. In the 1823 preface to the same work, he remarks that in it he has tried to solemnize some of the principal memories of his time which can be lessons for future societies. In 1824 the battle between Classicism and Romanticism became open, and Auger (1772– 1829), a Classicist critic, spoke out against the new movement which he called Romantic. Hugo did not take part in the battle, and even reproached the Romantics for some of their ideas. By 1826, however, Hugo had become a Romantic, but a prudent one who had not yet renounced his monarchist ideas. Romanticism was then narrow in scope: most of the artists who belonged to the movement believed it to be a joining of order and freedom. Liberty did not mean anarchy.

But by 1827 liberty became more important than order. This belief is found best expressed in Hugo's preface to *Cromwell* in which the poet sees the necessity of finding a leader to organize liberty. The concept of the genius who is the leader of men is first in evidence in this work, and Hugo now sees in Napoleon this sort of genius. The monarchy and organized religion are obstacles to the genius-leader, Hugo feels. By 1829 he had become the leader of poetic Romanticism, and his salon was the best known in Paris. The political metamorphosis that took place in Hugo, as in many of his contemporaries, was brought about by the stagnation and repression of the monarchy as well as the growing power of the bourgeoisie whose crass materialistic values and hypocritical sanctimoniousness offended him. Balzac's realistic portrayal of this group makes one understand the concern of the artists of the period and, as well, demonstrates the growing alienation between the creative artist and the society in which he lives. The conflict between the conservative, traditionalist middle class and the monarchy on one side and on the other the Romantics whose goal was political liberty and liberty in art was coming to a head.

The concept of liberty in art is best expressed in Hugo's preface to *Les Orientales* (1829). In it he proclaims the total independence of genius. Art for art's sake is his rallying cry. and it marks a complete change from his previous concern with politics and religion in art. Hugo's claim that art is the domain of beauty and that it should, of necessity, be divorced from morality makes him the father of the school of art for art's sake even though he later turned away from this doctrine. The necessity for proclaiming the freedom of the artist was evident to the young Romantics whose works had been attacked, often violently, by the academic and pedantic critics whose only standards of judgment were those of the previous century. Certain prose works escaped their anathema, as Rousseau's *La Nouvelle Héloise* and Chateaubriand's *Le Génie du christianisme* had earlier, because prose, and prose fiction especially, was not as rigidly controlled by rules as were the various forms of poetry and the theatre.

Yet a real revolution in poetical forms, techniques, and subject matter was slow in coming despite the claims of the Romantic poets. There is little except the sense of true sentiment and a subtle lyricism to differentiate the early poems of Lamartine from those of the neoclassical poets of the Empire. Hugo's several volumes of odes and ballads show a talented versifier but, with the exception of three or four poems, give little indication of the great poet he was to become. His subjects are basically those of poet laureates: occasional pieces on deaths, births, christenings, and the like. Only in some of the ballads is his true verbal and technical virtuosity seen. The early poems of the Romantics were in general well received, no doubt because they did not stray too far from accepted subject matter and traditional techniques. Among the successful works were the *Méditations poétiques* of Lamartine, the *Odes et ballades* of Hugo, and the *Poèmes antiques et modernes* of Vigny.

The real battle of Romanticism was, however, in the theatre. Drama, which is written to be presented before an audience, arouses more immediate reactions than a poem or a novel that is read in solitude, and acceptance by the public and critics is necessary for its success. The French theatre in the 1820's was dominated by productions of melodramas and bad neoclassical tragedies. The young Romantics attempted to revolutionize the most prestigious of the literary arts and attain acceptance of their plays in the national theatres, but they were thwarted by the strictly controlled policy of the government-appointed administrators and by the performers themselves who had been trained in the old tradition and were unwilling or unable to cope with the demands of the new plays.

Before looking at what the Romantics attempted to do in the theatre, it is necessary to discuss the characteristics of the Classical theatre against which they were revolting. The French Classical theatre is one of the glories of dramatic history. Corneille and Racine in tragedy and Molière in comedy produced an outstanding series of masterpieces from the production of *Le Cid* in 1637 to that of *Athalie* in 1691. Their plays spring from the same formal mold. The Classical drama has five acts and, with the exception of certain of Molière's comedies, is written in verse. Apart from the lyric choruses of Racine's biblical tragedies, the verse form is invariably the Alexandrine, a twelve-syllable line used in rhyming couplets. The regular Alexandrine has a caesura after the sixth syllable and a pause at the end of the line. Occasionally, for dramatic emphasis, lines are broken into three equally accented groups of four syllables each. Run-on lines or *enjambements* are extremely rare. The language of the play is "elevated" and contains none of the commonplaces or vulgarities of everyday speech. (Vigny was criticized in 1829 for using the word *mouchoir* [handkerchief] in his verse translation of Shakespeare's *Othello,* which demonstrates how ridiculous adherents of the formal style could become, for without the use of the handkerchief Othello's motivation becomes less dramatically plausible.) In Classical drama there is supposed to be no mixing of genres; tragedy must have no comic relief, and comedy should not have the overtones of tragedy. Molière's later plays often, and fortunately, depart from this doctrine, but then Molière, although a Classicist, was quite individualistic, a fact that perhaps explains why his plays met with success during the Romantic period and those of Corneille and Racine did not. The proper subject for tragedy was a man (or woman) of elevated stature struggling against an inexorable and predetermined fate; for comedy the portrayal of the foibles and vices of society. Comedies and tragedies alike observed the rule of the three unities of time, place, and action: A single plot must occur in one place within a period of twenty-four hours. In the Classical theatre, and especially in tragedy, there was little concern for verisimilitude in settings or costumes, and the actors used the declamatory style of speech.

Needless to say, with all these restrictions and conventions any dramatist but a genius would be stifled, and it is therefore not surprising that Classical drama in the eighteenth and early nineteenth centuries had become unimaginative and imitative. Voltaire alone stands out from among the numberless mediocrities who wrote tragedies in this period, and his plays, even at their best, are pale reflections of the masterpieces of Racine. Voltaire, however, was somewhat of an innovator in the theatre. He often used his plays as vehicles for his philosophical ideas, and in *Mahomet* provided a stirring attack on intolerance. His subjects were not all chosen from antiquity, and in *Alzire* he even used South America as the setting of the action. He absorbed much from Shakespeare but thought of the English poet as a barbarian, but a barbarian of genius, an idea that was reechoed even in the nineteenth century.

The eighteenth century produced two masters of comedy—Marivaux and Beaumarchais—but neither of them wrote in verse, and both broke the rules of Classical comedy. Marivaux's plays are comedies about the psychological complexities of love which he delicately portrays and analyzes. His plays are to the theatre what Fragonard and Watteau's canvasses are to painting. These exquisite comedies are the direct ancestors of the equally sensitive and delightful, although often more poignant, comedies of Musset, the master of the Romantic drama. Beaumarchais, influenced in part by the bourgeois drama of his epoch, created two of the great plays of the French theatre: *Le Barbier de Séville* (1775) and *Le Mariage de Figaro* (1784). His plays are essentially social comedies, full of wit and psychological penetration of character, but *Le Mariage de Figaro*, despite its overall air of good fun, is basically a revolutionary play. It is the first major comedy in France to attack the established political and social order, and its subject presaged the coming Revolution. Comedy, however, was not a major concern of the Romantic dramatists. Considered less prestigious than tragedy, it was not the means to make Romanticism triumph at the Comédie-Française. By a bizarre quirk of fate, however, it is the comedies of the Romantic era, and especially those of Musset, that have lasted as meaningful and absorbing works in the twentieth century. Most of the tragedies about which there was so much brouhaha in their time have disappeared from the boards except for occasional revivals as period pieces.

Before the many articles in the *Globe* and several other journals sympathetic to the cause of a Romantic theatre were published, the work that most resoundingly called for a new drama was the *Racine et Shakespeare* (1823) of Stendhal. Disappointed by the reception given a troupe of English actors performing Shakespeare the previous year, Stendhal decided to speak up for the admirers of the English bard and destroy the chauvinism characteristic of the French in general, and even of many of the young Romantics. Stendhal advises the young dramatist not to imitate Shakespeare's plays, but rather the way in which he studies the world because the world of the early nineteenth century resembles that of Shakespeare. Although he does not dismiss the writers of French Classical drama as useless, he does remark that the pleasure deriving from Classical tragedy is not that of the theatre but of the epic. For Stendhal the pleasure of the theatre lies in illusion, and nothing is more contrary to it than the use of verse and the unities. Therefore, Romantic tragedy must be a play in prose, freed from the unities of time and place, and the subject should come from national history. His ideas were, to a certain extent, illustrated by Mérimée and by Dumas in his *Henry III et sa cour* (1829).

The most important and influential call for a new theatre, however, is found in Hugo's preface to *Cromwell*. Hugo remarks that the evolution of poetry corresponds to the three stages of the history of mankind. Lyric poetry, exemplified by the Bible, is the product of primitive times. Epic poetry, typified by Homer, represents the heroic age. Drama is the poetry of modern times which are influenced by Christianity which has made man aware of his double nature—the spiritual and the physical. Shakespeare is his example of this type of poetry, and he concludes that drama is the form of art that best expresses the modern world. Hugo believes that it should be a faithful portrayal of life, that ugliness as well as beauty, the grotesque as well as the sublime, the comic as well as the tragic should be shown in drama. Dramatists should choose what is most characteristic of life, and since contrasts are a part of it they should be used to set each other off. Although Hugo, as opposed to Stendhal, wants drama to be written in verse, he also wants all the Classical restraints removed. He calls for a new vocabulary, new images, new techniques in the use of the Alexandrine, and a lack of reliance on the *bienséances*. The genres should be mixed as they are in quotidian life, and the unities of time and place abolished. Action should take place on the stage instead of being recounted by messengers and confidants. He calls, too, for historical truth in plot, settings, and costumes. And, perhaps most of all, he feels that the play should incarnate the thought of the poet and thus be a poetic treatment of reality. Hugo wrote several plays besides *Cromwell* to illustrate his thesis. Of these *Amy Robsart* (1828) failed and *Marion de Lorme* (1829) was forbidden by the censor. Yet that same year Dumas's *Henri III et sa cour* and Vigny's translation of *Othello* were produced at the Comédie-Française. The Romantic drama was beginning to make an impact.

Another major event that hastened the acceptance of Romantic drama was the successful extended tour of an English troupe of actors headed by Kemble and Miss Smithson (who later became Berlioz's wife). They gave a season (1827–28) of Shakespearean plays and were acclaimed by the Parisian public whose reaction was quite different than it had been five years previously, when another group of English actors presenting Shakespeare's plays had failed. The French, for one of very few times in their history, had forgotten chauvinism and acclaimed the genius of a foreign author. With the acceptance of Shakespeare, whose plays in no way resembled those of Racine and Corneille, the Romantic dramatists were encouraged by the possibility that their pieces would soon triumph as well. That triumph occurred on February 25, 1830, when *Hernani* was premiered at the

Comédie-Française. All the supporters of the new drama as well as the important defenders of the old were present, at the extremely raucous premiere. When the shouting was over not only *Hernani*, but Romanticism itself had triumphed. The way was now open for the production of Romantic plays, and many authors, including Nerval, hoped to make their fortune in the theatre.

Romanticism, as so many French literary movements, was given much impetus by the discussions in the salons of the 1820's. In many of the salons Anglophilia was the rage. Translations of Byron, Milton, and Shakespeare appeared, and an appreciative audience greeted them. *The Edinburgh Review,* which Byron had satirized in his "English Bards and Scotch Reviewers," was read with attention by many intellectuals. At the home of Delécluze, the art critic and student of David, one was likely to find Stendhal and Mérimée who also, with Delacroix and the actors Talma and Mlle Mars, appeared frequently at the salon of the painter Gérard. Artists, musicians, and writers mingled together in the salons and discussed the new aesthetic movement and its relation to all the arts which, each in its own way, were to interinfluence each other throughout the period. Balzac, Gautier, and Baudelaire became critics of art. Berlioz and Delacroix were men of literature as well as geniuses in their respective fields of music and painting. Nerval was an excellent music and theatre critic. The interrelation among the arts was, in part, due to the salons, one of the most important characteristics of Romanticism. In the salons artists from different media could discuss their aims, their ideals, and their concepts. Much of the descriptive literature of the epoch reflected the works of Delacroix and, a bit later, Daumier. Much of the lyricism of the period showed a fraternal bond with the melodies of Meyerbeer, Auber, and especially Berlioz whose exquisite settings of Gautier's poems in *Les Nuits d'été* and of Nerval's translations from *Faust* in *La Damnation de Faust* evinced a keen sense of the relationship between words and music. Romanticism in France appeared in all the arts simultaneously and not, as in England and Germany, in literature first and several decades later in painting and music.

The journals most important in their support of the Romantic

cause were *Les Tablettes universelles* (1820-24) and *Le Globe*.
The former was a cosmopolitan journal of politics and literature.
It contained, among others, articles on Lamartine and Walter
Scott and studies of Shakespeare. Basically a liberal paper, its
editorial pronouncements were essentially of the sort that said
that literature must keep up with politics; that is, that it must
be of its own times, as Stendhal had advocated in *Racine et
Shakespeare*. The viewpoint of the editors was, however, too
liberal for the repressive government of the restored monarchy,
and the paper was closed in 1824. It was succeeded by *Le Globe*,
which became the journalistic home of the new school for the
next five or six years. In its first number it presented a literary
manifesto in an effort to unite the past and present, tradition
and cosmopolitanism:

It remains for us to speak of our literary doctrines. Two words suffice:
liberty and respect for national taste. We shall applaud neither those
schools of germanicism or anglicism which menace the language of
Racine and Voltaire nor will we submit to the academic anathemas
of an outdated school which opposes to boldness only a worn-out
admiration and which endlessly invokes the glories of the past in
order to hide the misery of the present and only timidly observes
what the great masters have done, forgetting that the great masters
have been called such only because they were creators . . .[4]

Le Globe did not patronize any one literary school, and it
attempted to remain free of all attachments, yet its pages were
open to the Romantics as well as to representatives of other
literary beliefs. The importance of newspapers and journals
throughout the whole Romantic period was immense. Not only
did most of the greatest figures of the era write for them, but
many, like Balzac, Nerval, and Gautier earned their living
from them.

   Just what Romanticism was is difficult to define. Although
there are characteristics common to all the artists of the school,
there are, as well, many differences in their concepts of the
nature of art and of its function. Artistic liberty, a belief held
by the Romantics in general, implies, of course, differences in
subject matter, form, and technique, and the movement thus
was one of experimentation in which no two artists created

exactly alike. Individuality was the keynote of Romanticism, and its resultant masterpieces were created because the artists were not subject to an alien set of rigidly enforced aesthetic rules. Romanticism was "modern." Stendhal, in his *Racine et Shakespeare*, had declared that it was the art of presenting to contemporary people works susceptible of giving them the greatest possible pleasure. Classicism, he continued, gives them a literature that gave the greatest possible pleasure to their great-grandfathers. Thus, according to Stendhal, all works are "Romantic" in their own epoch but lose that quality when times change and new modes of expression are needed to portray them. Alexandre Guiraud, in an essay "Nos Doctrines" which appeared in *La Muse française,* claimed that contemporary literature should be a literature of the people rather than of scholars, a literature of inspiration rather than of memory—with an individual and intimate character. Emile Deschamps, in the preface of his *Études françaises et étrangères,* also believes in the relevance of literature to its time. He points out that one great literary century is never the continuation of another, that men of genius are always impelled toward the new, and the new in his century had been foreshadowed by the entry of poetry into prose in the works of Chateaubriand and Mme de Staël. Life and poetry are therefore needed in the new literature, but style, too, is important. For Deschamps style is composed of originality, movement, color, and individuality; since there are many ways of writing well, there are as many styles as there are authors.

In examining all the doctrines and manifestos of the 1820's, one remarks that the most characteristic elements of Romanticism are freedom, modernity, and lyricism. The artist is seen as an individual who should be true to his own nature rather than to rules, and thus he should express his ideas in the manner most appropriate to him. But defining Romanticism, instead of just giving its general characteristics, was as difficult for the Romantics as it is for us today. A witty woman of the period, the Duchesse de Duras, wrote on April 6, 1824, "The definition of Romantic is to be undefinable. It is an independent genre which takes its beauties wherever it finds them and believes only in itself. It is the Protestantism of literature, and like Protestantism it has many sects."[5] The great variety of Romantic works, ranging from the realism of Stendhal and Balzac to the lyricism of Hugo, from the philosophical and symbolic world of Vigny to the dream world of Nerval, from the sentimental art of Lamartine and the passionate outbursts of Musset to the Parnassian art of Gautier, is staggering. Occasionally one finds a theme such as that of the alienated hero or the rejected genius in many Romantic works that are otherwise different in style and form. But, generally speaking, each artist, using his own means of expression, sees life in different ways and presents the occupations of his epoch in ways that diverge in viewpoint from those of his contemporaries. Rather than a unified school, Romanticism is basically the sum of the products of myriad different subjective states of mind.

II *Nerval and the Romantic Movement*

Nerval's work is an artistic product of his own era, but the literary concepts found in his writings, as well as the forms that his ideas take, are often markedly different from those of his great contemporaries. Most Romantic writers, and one might say most writers in general, attempt to portray a visible world, one perceived by them optically, a world in which Nature and human nature are treated as realities. The portrayal of psychological as well as physical reality is a salient characteristic of the novels of Stendhal and Balzac. In the works of the poets Lamartine, Hugo, Vigny, Musset, and Gautier, the world is viewed and then portrayed in an effort to relate external reality to their own internal domain of emotions, ideas, and psychological forces. The reality thus presented in their works of art is generally fixed, as paint on a canvas; a vision, an idea, an emotion has been, in their best creations, pared artistically to its essential, and, although the poems may, and often do, cause reverberations beyond the confines of their immediate suggestions, they seldom evoke (with perhaps the exception of Hugo's prophetic works) an air of mystery or transcendence that opens unknown worlds to the intelligent reader.

Psychological complexity, as opposed to the simpler psychology of thwarted love, grief, despair, and alienation, is all but absent from their poems for, like their great seventeenth-century predecessors, they tend to see their feelings and their problems in general terms rather than in terms of the exceptional. The Romantic ego, even though it is personal and individual, tends to become generalized through the process of art. Vigny's sense of alienation is portrayed as the alienation of all superior beings. The gentle melancholy of Lamartine and the often frenetic despair of Musset, although personal in origin, become feelings that all humanity may experience while undergoing similar emotional problems. Even the great egotist Victor Hugo is the poet of the personal becoming the general. And access to their works is seldom difficult. These writers speak of a world we have either experienced or at least known to exist. Our pleasure in reading their poetry comes from a sense of familiarity with their subject matter and an admiration for the often novel way in which they have expressed it.

Nature, a dominant theme in Romanticism (although its importance has been overworked by too many generations of critics), is often viewed as a reflection of man's emotional world and may act as a consoler, guide, or friend. It may be, as in much of Vigny's poetry, hostile to man or, as in Hugo's, indifferent to him. But its presence is felt on the primary level of sensations and simple ideas. To many writers of the first half of the nineteenth century, Nature acts as a sort of divinity, and this fact accounts for the frequent pantheistic overtones in Romantic poetry and the consequent concept of the pathetic fallacy of Ruskin. But Nature, let it be remembered, is the world of the visible, the touchable, the auditory, the olfactory. It is a sensory presence and offers itself as such to man who may, consciously or unconsciously, draw correspondences between it and the private human world.

Nerval is less concerned than his contemporaries with Nature as such. His attempts to describe sylvan scenes or the tempests and furies of unleashed natural forces are seldom convincing in conventional terms. Lakes do not reflect his moods, nor do turbulent oceans, solitary mountains, or lush vegetation. Nature is there, of course, but it serves in his works more as a background, a theatrical setting, or a place name that evokes in the poet, much as it does later in the works of Proust, the memory of certain states of mind that may or may not have existed. This aberration from general Romantic thought lies in the psychological processes of Nerval's own mind. He creates or evokes a private world, a personal landscape, that transcends time and space. A flower is *the* flower, a tree *the* tree, a volcano *the* volcano. Nerval's is a world of absolutes, and he creates these absolutes by completely transforming and mythologizing the nonhuman and human worlds. His landscapes are seen obliquely. In his later works colors, sounds, and forms lack the basic function and balance one usually attributes to them because Nerval perceives them through a veil of memory, either real or imagined. The most striking aspect of his later poetry is the sense of tension between the contents of the sonnets and the form imposed on them, a form he rarely uses conventionally. A world of allusions, pauses, questions, emphases, a world that has lost its formal balance (as it does in the paintings of the Fauvists and Surrealists) is created in a way not seen before in French poetry.

Nerval himself with his own created personal mythology is the obsessive subject of both his poetic and prose masterpieces. His mythology, which will be discussed in more detail later, is peculiar to him. Lamartine, Vigny, Hugo, Musset, Gautier, and Baudelaire use conventional mythology for conscious parallels with the modern world, and their references to myth, history, and religion are generally clear for they are, or have become, part of the collective consciousness of humanity. In their works time is chronological and seldom fragmented; space is scientific and geographical. It is not the space of illusion become reality or memory become myth. Nerval's world is one of personal archetypes that have resonant, suggestive overtones to the reader, but it always retains an element of personal mysticism that cannot often be rationally explained.

Mysticism, of course, is an aspect of much of Romanticism.[6] The German and Scandinavian mystics and fabulists and the writings of men who belonged to the mystic societies of the eighteenth century and the period of the Empire were available to the French writers of the nineteenth century, and their influence can be seen in authors as different as Nodier and Balzac, Hugo and Baudelaire. But mysticism may take many forms, and most French Romantics dealt with the bizarre world of coincidence, magic, phrenology, astrology, alchemy, and pantheism in a rational way. None seems ever to have lived in a world in which the supernatural or the surreal took precedence over the quotidian world of reality. They may have believed in mystic dogmas, but they did not live them. Nerval did, and apparently had done so since he was a young child reading the works of eighteenth-century mystics that he had found in his uncle Antoine Boucher's attic. As he grew older Nerval tended more and more to live in a universe haunted by dreams, memories, and remembrances of his readings until the three tended to blend into one which became *the* reality, and it is of this reality that he wrote in most of his great works after his first mental crisis in 1841.

Nerval was an omniverous reader, and of all the major Romantics most likely had the greatest knowledge of books. Although his interests were many, the books that influenced him most were those of Goethe and the innumerable writings about the occult and primitive religions that he found either in Paris or had read in the library of Cairo. Goethe's influence can be seen from his earliest works in the 1820's to the *Aurélia* of 1854. Nerval gives the impression of feeling that he is the double of Faust. Like him, the poet seeks the ideal woman, a search which leads him into a world of archetypes with whom he identifies. His constant seeking for himself and knowledge of the universe that is denied most men parallels the quest of Faust as well. Like his fictional German counterpart, the French poet wants, through knowledge and often by use of the occult sciences, to penetrate the mysteries that keep him from the perception of a unity that exists behind the discordant appearances of reality. This quest was greatly influenced by the use of the writings of the Illuminists in which he found some of the principal ideas he would later use in *Aurélia*. The Illuminists produced an occult philosophy which resembled in many ways the doctrines of the mystic Swedenborg. Man, as seen by the Illuminists, has been placed in a world of symbols. He must learn to develop his latent faculties, to disengage his *moi intérieur* which these mystics called "the divine spark," and, if necessary, to use occult means to interpret these symbols in order to enjoy that intuition, based on spiritual illumination, that would not only provide knowledge of the self but of the universe as well, and put man into contact with the inhabitants of the invisible world. *Aurélia* is, in a sense, the story of Nerval's quest for such a spiritual illumination. However, in order to achieve it, he had not only to disengage his interior self from external reality, but to rely on cabalistic lore. He writes, "My role seemed to me to be to reestablish universal harmony by cabalistic art and seek a solution by evoking the occult forces of different religions."[7] Much of his knowledge of religion comes from the work of a German author Frederick Creuzer, *Les Religions de l'antiquité*. But other works as well were retained in his memory and become part of his own personal mysticism.

An important element of this mysticism is his creation of a personal mythology which, whether or not it is essentially a product of his states of madness, becomes a reality in his literary works. This mythology often mirrors what appear to be schizophrenic problems in the personality of the poet. At various points in his life, and especially after the breakdown of 1841, Nerval identified with different heroes and divinities such as Osiris, Napoleon, Adoniram, Caliph Hakem, and the Cainites, children of fire. His attempts to create for himself a glorious geneology (the Roman emperor Nerva, Napoleon) evidences an attempt at self-aggrandizement and betrays an inferiority complex which is also suggested in his changing of his name from Gérard Labrunie to Gérard de Nerval. That he identifies with those who either failed in this life or were outcasts from it is not surprising, for he, too, like them, was alienated from the material world in his dreams and hoped that he would achieve the perfection and knowledge that they had in the spiritual world. The destructive aspect of the myth is found in Nerval's renouncing of our everyday reality for one that was more tenuous, one approaching the world of madness. The constructive part of the myth is the literary works produced by the mind of the man who lived it.

But if Nerval is always the major male character in his personal mythology, there are many females who eventually coalesce into one great goddess who is a composite of real women he had known and divinities from ancient religions. Death had separated the women he loved most from him: his mother had died a year and a half after his birth; Adrienne, a childhood sweetheart, had died in a convent; Jenny Colon, the actress and perhaps the greatest love of his life, had died young. These dead women who were no longer in his life presented no threat to his mythic dream, and they were soon identified with the Virgin Mary, Isis, and the Queen of Sheba in the form of the all-loving female goddess through whose intercession he might attain salvation and knowledge. Unlike his contemporaries, Nerval did not just identify with his myths, he lived them.

The obsessive form that myth takes in his life and works is quite different from that of the other Romantic authors. Vigny, Lamartine, and Hugo use myth as a frame of reference for their readers in order to communicate their ideas, but the myths they use are accessible to their public for, one might say, they are in the public domain. What is of importance in their use of myth is how they reinterpret it, how they make it relevant to their times. Nerval, on the other hand, although he does use certain well-known myths, usually combines them with more esoteric and lesser-known myths of the non-Judaic middle eastern tradition. To these are added the personal myths discussed above, myths developed in his mind over a period of years that are often based on events in his past or more often are romanticized or created memories of his childhood in the Valois and his amorous experiences in the 1830's. To these are added personal views of actual historical figures of whose lives he creates mythical material. All these forms of myth used separately, in combinations, or in juxtapositions, lead the reader through a dizzying experience in which accepted frames of reference no longer exist. Thus, many of his works tend to be hermetic, difficult to understand, and yet they remain evocatively rich. If the art of poetry is that of suggestion rather than statement, then Nerval must be counted among the master poets of the nineteenth century.

Of the Romantic poets Nerval is the one who most consistently describes a personal world that is often alien, although always fascinating, to many readers whose experiences have not led them into a state of mind of almost constant fantasy and dreams with their consequent transformations of reality. Most writers describe or portray aspects of their personality, their mental landscapes, in their works. An artist's way of viewing his world, experiencing it, and then portraying it in his works is, of course, his own, and the great artist differs from the minor one in this very act. But the greatest writers are somehow able to make their world coincide with general human experience so that the readers feel that he is part of that world or, at least, has experienced aspects of it himself. Thus, in the works of most great artists the personal becomes universal, expressing but transcending its intimate source. These writers may, in their works, create a new reality, but it is a reality that is easily grasped by the public which, because of this new means of presenting the human condition, may perceive new elements and aspects of life.

Through constant rereading and often with a willing suspension of disbelief, the reader of Nerval's works will find a new reality, the reality of the dream and its relations with man's subconscious. Yet this reality borders on the mystical, if not the magical, for Nerval's writings deal almost exclusively with himself and the nonrealistic world he has created for himself to live in. When Nerval tries to communicate on a basic literary level, as in his plays and fiction, he becomes banal, a fact proved by the history of his theatrical failures. Only in the works which express what today we would call the surreal or supernatural world, a world of emblems and signs that have meaning for Nerval alone, do we recognize the individuality and power of a great artist who is presenting a reality that may be beyond our immediate ken, but one that we know exists.

The very ambivalence of the "I" in Nerval's works is enough to deroute the perceptive reader. Since so much of his literature is written from an apparently autobiographical viewpoint, one tends to see his masterpieces such as *Sylvie, Voyage en Orient, Aurélia,* and *Les Chimères* as autobiographical accounts of his past. But the "I" who participated in these past events experiences them in the present, and the remembered reality is somehow transformed into the present fantasy of what the past was, and much of it is invented. So, in reading works such as *Sylvie, Octavie, La Pandora,* and *Aurélia,* the reader must remember that a knowledge of Nerval's life, while useful, is not always indispensable. The "I" who recounts the stories is more often relating fiction, in the created sense, than fact. Nerval creates and exaggerates himself in the present while supposedly describing himself in the past. What he sees, of course, is momentary reality to him, but this reality is the result of the myths he has mentally created and nourished throughout his life until he has come to believe in their existence as well as their truth. Myth to Nerval, however, does not mean the same thing as it does to other men who recognize myths as expressions of the human predicament rather than as escapes from it. Nerval spent much of his life creating myths both of himself and of the women he loved, but their true significance is locked in the poet's mind and does not have the universal connotations that myths ordinarily do.

Yet given a lack of universality in Nerval's created myths, there is still one myth which he experiences that is related to all men—the myth of quest. All of his major works are works of quest—quest for reality, for salvation, for self. And, because of the very humanity, the anguish, and only occasionally the joys caused by the quest, we find in Nerval's works a reality that is close to our own, for his great and central character, his created self, reflects many of our own states of mind. It is thus not as an eccentric nor as a man prone to madness (he was both) that Nerval should be studied, but as a human with an extraordinary perception of worlds beyond rational consciousness who, having failed in life, attempted to find in uncharted worlds beyond it the secrets of existence in the deepest recesses of the mind.

To his friends Nerval was a Romantic writer with a Romantic mentality. He had participated in the battle of *Hernani*, had translated Goethe's *Faust*, had written Romantic plays with Alexandre Dumas, père, had shared their identification with, and love of, the music of Meyerbeer, had written, and wrote throughout most of his mature life, literary and musical criticism that seemed to his contemporaries (if not to us today) to extol the Romantic movement, had a great fascination for the Middle East (what the Romantics called the Orient), and a moderate interest in the political events of the day. He also believed ardently in the importance of love. Yet if all these aspects are characteristic of Romanticism in general, each took a different form both in Nerval's own psychology as well as in his works.

His participation, and Gautier's as well, in the battle of *Hernani* was more the bravado and attention-attracting desire of a young man whose cause, if he genuinely had one, had not yet been clearly defined. His interest in Germany and its literature was genuinely felt, for he found in the country across the Rhine a land of legends and myths, a land of mysticism which appealed to his love of the occult and the bizarre. Of all the Romantic poets, Nerval had the deepest understanding, even though it was mainly intuitive, of the Teutonic mind. His discovery of Goethe and subsequent translation of *Faust* was one of the most important events of his psychological as well as literary life, for in the works of the German master Nerval found a spiritual brother whose quest was to become his own. The elements of mystery and magic that the French poet found in German literature, themes that one rarely finds in French Romantic poetry, were to become integral parts of his own work because of his obsession with the spiritual and the occult.[8]

An interest he shared with Sainte-Beuve was French poetry of the Renaissance whose influence is seen in his own early verses. In fact, much of the intimate quality as well as the form of Nerval's poetry can be traced to the poems of the Pléiade which he helped to reinstate in the accepted literary canon. The lightness of touch and the insouciant quality of some of Nerval's youthful poetry come, however, not only from the sixteenth-century poets, but, as well, from his love of his native province, the Valois, and its landscapes which later are so charmingly depicted in *Sylvie*. The works Nerval wrote in the 1830's also reflect the bohemianism of his life in this decade. His *vie de Bohème*, however, was hardly that depicted by Murger, for Nerval did not lack for money during much of this decade, and his extravagances and hedonism were more those of the dandy than of the struggling artist. He writes of these years which were among the happiest of his life in *Petits Châteaux de Bohème*. Although Nerval is essentially a product of the city, one finds in his works an overpowering nostalgia for the countryside in which he spent his childhood. The Valois, like Germany and later Naples, takes on a mystical aura, in part through the process of memory, and becomes associated in his mind with a sort of purity and innocence that was not to be found in Paris.

Although Nerval wrote many plays and was much influenced by the theatre, none of them has survived on today's stages and few were ever presented at all. Yet the magic of theatre fascinated him throughout his life, in no small part owing to his unsuccessful love for the actress Jenny Colon who incarnated for him the fascination of the stage. Like most of the Romantics, he wanted above all to succeed in the theatre, but, unlike his contemporaries, he transmitted his sense of the theatrical in his prose works where Nature becomes an artifice, a theatrical setting in which his dreams and fantasies unfold. The world is a stage, in the literal sense of the term, in Nerval's works, but it is a stage with a fabulous décor on which one real person, the author, and many phantoms play out their parts. The view of the world as theatrical is found again in certain of Rimbaud's prose poems and in Proust's *A la recherche du temps perdu,* but in the latter work, despite the artifice of the settings, the characters come alive because of Proust's objective portrayal of their tics, manias, and follies. Nerval, like Julien Sorel in Stendhal's *Le Rouge et le noir,* creates situations, settings, and characters only to have them fade away into dreams. But for Nerval the dreams are reality and what he ends with is a series of ghost sonatas in which the dream is indistinguishable from the vague reality it is supposed to represent. The only reality is what the author chooses to see, not what is there.

Nerval earned much of his livelihood from writing critical articles about the literary and musical events of his time. Although many of the obsessions found in his creative works reappear in his criticism, Nerval's critical writings give evidence of an original and independent mind. Individual works of art interest him more than schools, and, despite his fervor for certain Romantic works, he is well aware of the beauties and values of the writings of Classicism. When he deals in his articles with contemporary works, he is much more perceptive than Sainte-Beuve who never really understood the genius of a Balzac or a Hugo. Nerval delights in the diversity of the literature of his epoch and faithfully presents both its characteristic traits and its originality. On a level with the criticism of Balzac and Gautier and a bit below that of Baudelaire, Nerval's critical journalism shows him to be one of the most inspired critics of his era.

His interest in the Middle East went far deeper than that of most of his contemporaries who were interested in it for either political or humanitarian reasons or as a source of local color for their writings. The Orient for Nerval was the home of mysticism, of seemingly defunct mythologies, of the race of pre-Adamites and Cainites with whom he identified. His Orientalism was often that of the descriptive and not always original travel diary, but more often it was that of an initiate into religions far beyond the interest or comprehension of his great contemporaries. Later we shall see that sections of his *Voyage en Orient* are among the most startling pieces of prose writing in Romantic literature.

The importance of the theme of love in the Romantic period cannot be overestimated. No longer could it be described, as Chamfort did in the eighteenth century, as the contact of two epidermises and the exchange of two fantasies. Nor was it the simple satisfaction of sensual desire. Love was an ideal to the Romantics, one that could not always be attained, but toward which one strove. The concept of woman, which differed greatly from author to author, defined an artist's view of love. Vigny was a misogynist, and it is therefore not surprising that love plays a small role in his works. But women did inspire love in most of the authors. Some, such as Mme de Staël and George Sand, wrote of the "new" woman who was the equal of man, and this type of woman was beloved of authors such as Schlegel and Shelley. The *femme fatale* who inspired desperation as well as love in men is found in the works of Musset, Mérimée, and Baudelaire. Woman was also seen as the representative of purity, in the tradition of Dante's Beatrice and Petrarch's Laura; she was an angel who ennobled, inspired, encouraged, and saved man. Representing the fusion of love and religion, she is found in the works of Goethe, Lamartine, Hugo, and especially Nerval. Hugo, who was a satyr in his personal life, portrays love not as a sexual impulse or a caprice of the heart, but rather as a divine principle. As such, it was more powerful than social traditions and the law. This concept can be seen in his plays *Hernani* and *Ruy Blas*. For Nerval, however, love was the directing force of his life and work both before and after his encounter with Jenny Colon. In his personal life, the women he loved, as opposed to desired, were unobtainable and therefore his love turns into myth. This creation of the myth of the ideal woman, peculiar in its many manifestations to Nerval, is not found again in French literature until the poems of the Surrealists.

For Nerval the beloved exists on an ethereal plane, and communion is only possible on a platonic level. Nerval's great work *Aurélia* demonstrates the near-Gidian distinction between physical desire and love. Reticent about his sexual life and tormented by guilt for having submitted to the pleasures of the flesh, Nerval (and later Baudelaire) had a horror of the body and its imperfections. A dichotomy thus evolves in his works between the body and the spirit, and, although Nerval was hardly a devout or even practicing Catholic, there is much in his concept of love, of the flesh, of the spiritual that is reminiscent of early Christian saints and mystics such as St. Augustine and St. Theresa of Avila. But Nerval is constantly haunted by the thought of loss, of failure, of damnation, be it in the world of the Christian God or in the polytheistic world of his own lived imagination. In his essay on Heinrich Heine's *Intermezzo* in 1848, Nerval writes:

In Faust one will even find love impregnated with supernaturalism; but the patient and sickly analysis of an ordinary love, without contrasts and without obstacles, drawing from its own substance what makes it painful or fatal—that is what belongs to a nature in which nervous sensibility predominates . . .[9]

The love of which he is speaking is a characteristic of, as well as a product of, the Judeo-Christian tradition, and Nerval finds that Heine is the victim of it. But he might as well be speaking about himself.

In Romantic literature women may well be idealized, but they are generally creatures of flesh and blood. In the works of Nerval woman is more a transcendent presence like the Châtelaine, in his poem "Fantaisie," "in her high tower, blond with

dark eyes, in her old-fashioned clothes, whom in another existence, perhaps, I have already seen . . . and whom I remember."[10]
She exists in memory, as does Aurélia, and to a lesser extent
Adrienne, Sylvie, and Octavie. There is a peculiarly virginal
quality about the women in Nerval's works and hence they are
inaccessible to him. Perhaps for this reason Nerval creates the
myth of the goddess-mother who is a combination of the women
he had known and loved and the divinities of different religions.
Very seldom in his works does he give an incidence of consum-
mated physical love, and when he does, as in the case of Adoniram and the Queen of Sheba, it has been preordained from the
beginning of time. Yet Nerval was human and had very human
desires which he evidently tried to suppress, and when he
failed to do so felt a strong sense of guilt. In an essay on tragedy
the author wrote, "A tragic heroine must be an example of
chastity or a model of shamelessness. Iphigenia and Phaedra—
there's no middle ground."[11] Nerval thus classifies women into
two groups, and he is obsessed by both "the sighs of the saint
and the screams of the fairy." There was no permanent escape
from his dilemma, and the tension caused by it is found in much
of his best work and was perhaps a cause of his recurrent bouts
with madness.

If one were to choose the most enigmatic, difficult, and fascinating poet of the nineteenth century, the choice would have to
be between Nerval and Rimbaud, the latter because his genius
produced in a few years some of the finest and most evocative
poetry in the French language. But Rimbaud's works after the
age of twenty-five amount to little more than his correspondence.
Nerval's finest works were a product of steady artistic growth
and were all published in the last four years of his life. In these
works Nerval crosses and recrosses boundaries not between
artistic vision and the human reality on which it is based, but
boundaries which go beyond those of the normal artistic imagination, that is to say, into a world of madness, not the divinely
inspired madness spoken of by writers since the beginning of
recorded literature, but true madness in which an author creates
a world that is alien to other men, a world over which he alone
reigns. Fortunately for us, Nerval was able to return from his
chimerical land of insanity to his everyday reality and describe

or suggest the mysteries that lie beyond. Yet his awareness that at any moment he might be forced back into that world which other men consider one of madness took its toll in his mental state and led directly to his suicide. He was not a Holderlin, who went insane permanently, nor a Rimbaud who could induce hallucinations if not outright states of madness by artificial means. He often led a dual life, a possible victim of schizophrenia, and he was terrified of it because he could not control it. His adventures in the world of dreams, of madness, and of reverie are the subjects of his literary works, and they demonstrate that although he was of the Romantic era he was not always consciously in it.

CHAPTER 2

The Poet

ALTHOUGH Nerval is considered primarily a poet by most readers, it is surprising to note that, apart from his poetry of adolescence and lyrics for opera libretti, he wrote only about fifty poems. Of these, two are close adaptations of poems by Thomas Moore, one a translation of an aria from Donizetti's *Anna Bolena,* one an imitation of a poem by Uhland, and three are reworkings or different versions of other poems. Nerval's poetry varies in quality from some uninspired and unoriginal poems in the style made fashionable by the early works of Lamartine and Hugo to the masterpieces of *Les Chimères.*

Nerval's poetic activity was basically concentrated in two short periods of his life—the early 1830's and the early 1850's. Before 1831, when he was twenty-three, his output consisted of his adolescent poetry, the "Pensée de Byron," the "Stances élégiaques," the imitations, adaptations, and the translation of Part I of Goethe's *Faust.* His first significant original poetry, twelve poems in all, appeared in 1831–32. Nothing is recorded for the next two years, and between 1835 and 1839, in addition to the lyrics for *Paquillo,* only four poems were written. In 1842 he wrote a poem of thanks to Victor Hugo. From 1843 to 1845 three of the *Chimères* and four other poems were written. The remainder of his poetry was written from 1852 to January, 1855. Nerval's poetic development is of much interest, and I shall study the poetry chronologically, beginning with the early poems including the *Odelettes* and then study *Les Chimères.*

I The Early Poems

Written in 1827, the poem "Pensée de Byron" shows Nerval's early infatuation for the English poet whose *Lara* he was to adapt for the theatre several years later. This poem of two stanzas of eight octosyllabic lines contains no startling imagery.

38

The subject is disappointment in love and already contains a premonition of the poet's subsequent amorous failures. The language is basically banal:

Through my love and constancy I'd thought to make your hardness give way. And the breath of hope had entered my heart. But time, which I prolong in vain, has taught me the truth. Hope has fled like a dream, and only my love remains.[1]

In the second stanza love is compared to an abyss between the poet's life and happiness, to a sickness of which he is the victim, and to a weight cast on his heart. This poem of despair could easily be dismissed as typical mediocre writing of the epoch were it not for the fact that Nerval shows a good rhythmic sense, and the subject is one that was to haunt him throughout his life. One might question the poet's sincerity and ask whether he was just striking a pose fashionable in the years immediately following Byron's death in 1824. The answer remains unknown, but the fact that much of Nerval's life was a reliving of a similar amorous distress tends retrospectively to give the poem a biographical importance that it does not deserve aesthetically.

The "Stances élégiaques" of 1829 contains two elements that are important in the development of Nerval's poetry: the use of irony and poignant imagery to reflect the mood of the poet. The irony is found in the first stanza in which the poet portrays a lovely stream reflecting the sunny skies. Underneath, however, it is poisoned by pollution. Nerval then compares to himself this image of purity with corruption at its source. Outwardly he may smile, but his heart is of ice because of a memory (which is not related to the reader) that has removed all hope from his life. The last stanza contains a striking image:

When the dried up branch, half detached from the tree trunk by the black Southern winds, sees again the fine days of spring; if sometimes a moving ray of sun wandering over its sterile head makes its naked branches shine it smiles in the light, but springtime greenery will not be reborn on its face.[2]

Aside from the Germanic overtones of the subject matter which cause one to think of texts Schubert set to music, there is a deep sense of anguish in the poem that is remarkable for so young a poet to have experienced. Perhaps there is an element of Romantic posturing, but the poet does convince us of his sincerity. This can be seen in the power of the mysterious "memory drenched with tears that overwhelms (him) and spreads its shadow over (his) pleasures and griefs."[3] The mysterious quality—something suggested but not explained—has overtones of the mystery of the Byronic heroes. Yet here again is one of Nerval's lifelong obsessions: guilt. The memory could be related to the death of the poet's mother or, more probably, to problems with early loves, but these interpretations add little to the poignancy of the poem or to the mysterious quality of the poet's sadness. The idea of being tainted, polluted like the stream, suggests much to the reader's imagination. One wonders whether the memory is important because of something the poet himself has done and for which he feels a hopeless guilt. Certainly the image of the befouled stream would indicate this possibility. A similar obsessive guilt is found in many of Nerval's later works, especially in *Aurélia*, and it is often related to remorse after a sexual encounter. The use of the words "filth," "impure," and "stain" have both physical and psychological connotations. Their effect is strong and add to the poem's final mood of despair.

Nerval's best early poems were written between 1830 and 1832. In these works Nerval became a minor master of poetry of suggestion rather than statement and, as well, a consummate technician. The technical brilliance of these poems can be readily seen in "Les Papillons" (1830–33) in which the poet uses the *vers impair* (a line with an uneven number of syllables) to fine effect. Although not quite so superb an example of technical mastery or showmanship as Hugo's "Les Djinns," this poem still is remarkable for its unity of subject and form. "Les Papillons" is in three parts of which the first two consist of four stanzas each. The first and third stanzas have six lines of 7, 3, 3, 3, 3, 7 syllables respectively, with a rhyme scheme of aabccb. The musicality of the close rhymes and the consequent rapid movement of the lines suggest the lightness and capriciousness of the butterflies:

> The butterfly, stemless flower,
> Which flutters,

That one gathers in a net:
In infinite nature,
Harmony
Between plant and bird![4]

The second and fourth stanzas consist of eight seven-syllable lines with the rhyme scheme ababcdcd which contrast well in rhythm with the first and third stanzas.

Although the poet's presence as an observer of various types of butterflies is important in the first two parts of the poem, a personal note is found in the third part, which is exactly half as long as the first two. After a remarkable lepidopteral description, the poet suddenly sees the dangers to these stemless flowers. They can be caught and, ironically, mounted by an innocent child: "A very young girl with a tender heart and gentle smile, piercing your hearts with a needle, contemplates you with surprise...."[5] The theme of the poem is that innocence hurts. The agility and grace of this odelette (a light ode rather than a serious or dramatic one) shows the influence of Ronsard on the nineteenth-century poet, an influence found in much of Nerval's early poetry.

It is seen again in one of Nerval's most successful poems—the exquisite "Avril" of 1831. In subject matter this odelette seems reminiscent of the opening of T. S. Eliot's "The Waste Land."[6] Most poets have praised the month of April, the month of renaissance. Nerval, however, sees it as a prelude to spring. The poem is ambiguous for it is not clear whether the poet is writing it in March and describing April which will soon arrive or describing April from the vantage point of April looking forward to May. In 1835, perhaps to clear up the ambiguity, the poem was republished under the title *Odelette—March 25.*

In the first stanza, which begins with the adverb "already," as if time had made a sudden impression on him, the poet tells us that fine weather has arrived:

Already beautiful days, dust, an azure and sunny sky, sun-hit walls, long evenings; And nothing green: scarcely yet does a reddish reflection adorn the large trees with black branches![7]

The sun may be strong enough to cause a fiery glow on light-colored walls, but it casts only a slightly reddish tinge on the black branches. The first stanza of "Avril" is descriptive; it contains nine adjectives and only one verb, which is descriptive in quality. The poet himself is a passive observer except in his implicit comments shown by the temporal adverbs "already" and "scarcely yet." The rhyme scheme is a favorite of Nerval—aabccb, a rhyming couplet followed by *rimes embrassées*—a scheme far more lyrical than a series of rhyming couplets.

In the second stanza, the poet himself enters the poem. He remarks that the "fine weather oppresses and annoys (him),"[8] a mood reminiscent of Baudelaire's "L'Automne," but the two poets part company in their respective sentiments. More than any other Romantic poets, both are deeply affected by the weather, but Nerval, tired of winter, is impatient for full-fledged spring. Baudelaire is depressed because autumn is tolling the death knell of summer and winter is his arid season, his season of spiritual and creative death. Nerval, in a state of depression, awaits the end of rainy days for only then will "spring, pink and becoming green, burst forth in a tableau like a newly born nymph who comes smiling out of the water."[9] Whereas the first stanza is descriptive, the second with its six verbs has more action and movement. The rhythmic variety of the octosyllabic lines of "Avril" is seen in Nerval's use of the caesuras which change from line to line and are found after either the third, fourth, or fifth syllable. For example, in the first line "Déjà les beaux jours, la poussière," the caesura comes after "jours" (the fifth syllable). There is a resultant heaviness in "la poussière" which contrasts with the rest of the line and consequently and implicitly expresses the author's feeling about the dust. The harshness and starkness of the primary colors in the first stanza (red, black, blue) give way to the pastel colors of the second, and parallel the mellowing of the poet's mood. "Avril" is one of Nerval's most perfect poems.

"Politique" (1831) is a poem of gentle irony commenting on one of Nerval's brief stays in prison. Although only carousing with friends, Nerval was arrested for trying to overthrow the government. The charges were dismissed, but this poem, reminiscent of those of Charles d'Orléans, resulted from the event. Here again one finds the writer's lyric and rhythmic gifts. His use in each stanza of three lines of six syllables and the fourth of four, with the rhyme scheme aabb, gives both a sense of poignancy and a pointedness to his ideas. This effect is amplified in the first stanza by four rhymes with a dominant "i" sound which express a sense of despair that is later modified in the poem.[10] In "Politique" there is a contrast between confinement in prison and the freedom of the natural world outside. The poet thirsts for "something green before winter comes,"[11] for some sign of life to assuage his sadness, to make him confident that a nature and a God exist outside.

Another poem of the same year is "Le Point noir" (originally entitled "Le Soleil et la gloire"), an adaptation of a sonnet by the German poet Burger. Nerval had originally translated it into French prose, and it was published in his *Poésies allemandes* in 1830. This poem is quite close in language to the prose translation. Its importance is not in its originality, but in Nerval's choice of a subject that had much appeal for him. The "point noir" is a symbol of failure, of an awareness of the poet's own limitations. The symbol is then broadened to include all of humanity: "Only the eagle—woe betide us all—contemplates with impunity the Sun and Fame."[12] The same despondency is also found in "Laisse-moi" (1831), but it is more pronounced. The twenty-three year old poet thinks of himself as being old and asks a young girl if she cannot see that "in (his) sadness, (his) pale and youthless brow must no longer smile at happiness."[13] Even if she loved him she could not banish his melancholy. The tone of the poem is again similar to Baudelaire's "Automne," which was written nearly a quarter of a century later. For both poets love is a good emotion, but other things are more important, and love cannot dispel these pressures from the poet's mind. In the fourth stanza there is a noteworthy inversion of a Romantic metaphor:

But now, o girl, your glance is the star that shines in the troubled eyes of sailors whose bark is about to be shipwrecked. At the moment when the storm ceases it breaks and disappears under the waves.[14]

The star would ordinarily represent hope, but for Nerval, even in his earliest works, the star, as in the later "El Desdichado" and *Aurélia,* is one of despair and melancholy.

Perhaps the most famous of Nerval's early poems is "Fantaisie" (1832). In this work of extraordinary technical felicity certain obsessions that reappear in most of his later writings are found. "Fantaisie" was reprinted in 1834 under the title "Souvenirs d'une autre vie," in 1840, in 1842 with the title "Vision" and dedicated to Gautier, and again in the same year in *L'Artiste* with the title "Odelette." It is one of his key poems as well as one of the best. The decasyllabic line is used to perfection, and, at the age of twenty-four, his handling of poetic form and diction shows him to be already a master. The rhyming is irregular: In the first stanza the poet uses *rimes embrassées,* in the other three *rimes croisées.*

The poem is basically one of correspondences and a definite forerunner of Proust's theory of involuntary memory. It begins with a general statement, "There is an air for which I would give all Rossini, all Mozart, and all Weber."[15] The melody is described as being very old, languishing, and funereal. The key to the poem is found in the fourth line when Nerval relates that it has "secret charms for (him) alone."[16] The expression "for me alone" recurs frequently in the writer's works and is indicative of the solitary and unique experiences he underwent as well as his desire to place them in a realm of myth and magic that has a special significance only for him. The association of the melody with a pleasing event suggests a privileged moment, an epiphany at some time in the past, a moment which can be recalled and enjoyed in the present. Each time the poet hears the melody, his soul grows "two hundred years younger."[17] He is thus living simultaneously on two different temporal levels. Immediately a visual image of the epoch of Louis XIII appears. The poet *believes* (there is a possibility of doubt implied) he sees a green slope made golden by the setting sun, a brick château with stone corners and pane glass windows tinged with reddish colors. The château is surrounded by large parks, and there is a river that flows among flowers bathing the foot of the château. Nerval then perceives a lady in a high window, a lady with blond hair and brown eyes in a dress of other days, a lady he has perhaps seen in another existence and whom he remembers. But there is always the element of doubt. Did she really exist except in the poet's fancy? If so, then fancy is as real, or perhaps more real, than reality itself. Myth becomes not only an expression of reality, but reality itself.

The poem thus develops from a personal statement about the melody and its effects on the poet to the description of a past time and place which become the setting for the beautiful woman of the last verse. The poem ends with another personal and discreet statement about the poet and the woman. On reading the poem, one is instantly struck by the multiple references to time—most of them imprecise or general and consequently quite suggestive (ancient, each time, two hundred years [an approximation], Louis XIII [suggestive of an historical period], grow younger, sunset, yellows, old-fashioned clothes, in another existence, already, I remember). Each of the last three stanzas begins with a temporal expression, but time does not progress: It *is*. Past and present intermingle, become one for the poet in the privileged moment. Yet there is uncertainty whether this moment ever existed except in the present or in the imagination. This idea is indicated by the expressions "I think I see," "perhaps I saw," "in another existence." The poem, however, ends affirmatively with "and I remember." No doubt is expressed. But if time is one, it is so only in the imagination. Nerval is negating chronological time, and it therefore becomes psychologically all-important, for the poet by dismissing it makes his retreat into the imagination all the more poignant. The fact that only the time of the imagination has aesthetic and psychological value for the poet is a key point which Nerval will later use to great advantage and with equal felicity in *Les Chimères*.

"Fantaisie" is the earliest poem of Nerval in which the problem of illusion and reality has major importance. The poet's awareness at the age of twenty-four of psychological time, a flux in which he immersed himself more and more in later years, and which has no little bearing on his spells of madness, is already evident in "Fantaisie." Myth, personal and racial, which later obsesses him in both his life and works, is already evident here in the almost worshipful tone of his description of the blond lady with brown eyes. It is not, therefore, surprising to find the physical distance between the poet and the lady. There are no sexual undertones in the poem. The lady is

at her window; the poet is looking up at her. Thus, above him
and apparently unobtainable, she can be adored.

Although "Fantaisie" is not a poem of despair, there is a
touch of sadness, a note of melancholy in the adoration which,
as the dots (...) indicate, cannot be captured in present reality,
but only in present remembered time. The poet *thinks* he sees
the scene. The music which evokes the memory is old, languishing, and funereal. The first adjective sets the time; the second
gives not only the tone and effect of the music, but of the
memory and the poem itself. There is just the slightest hint
of sensuality, but it is in pastel colors. "Funereal," however,
evokes other connotations. Was the music funereal or did the
remembered event have funereal overtones which the poet
identifies with the music? The implication is that the memory
evoked by the lady had sad implications—perhaps her very in-
accessibility—which are suggested but not stated. The melody
transcends time, but it can be perceived only in the imagination,
a reality different from that of the audible music. The music
has charms for Nerval alone, and the word "alone" is emphasized
at the caesura. The element of mysteriousness of the poem is
enhanced by the use of the words "secret charms." Just as
Rimbaud in "Parade" claims that he alone has the key to the
mystery, Nerval is so personally involved in his fantasy that he
alone can explain its charms. The title of the poem was originally
"Fantaisie," which means imagination, fantasy in the Cole-
ridgean sense. The title, thus, too, poses the question of reality.
Two years later (1834) the title became "Memories of Another
Life" which is more specific, but still evocative. In 1842, after
Nerval's first internment for madness, the poem was retitled
"Vision"—a significant change, for this title suggests the mystic
which the earlier two do not.

Of the other poems published in 1832, "Romance" is a fine
translation of Smeaton's aria "Deh non voler constingere a finta
gioia il viso" from the first act of Donizetti's *Anna Bolena*. Anna
has been replaced in Henry VIII's favor by Jane Seymour and
is the victim of great anguish. Smeaton, to console her, sings
her this aria. It is not surprising that it should have appealed
to Nerval, for Anna, whether sad or happy, is to her musician
Smeaton a goddess who has awakened the first fires of love.

Her unhappiness parallels Nerval's for, as he says in "Stances élégiaques," his smiles only hide his tears. Nerval identifies both with Anna and with Smeaton, with her because of her predicament and her attitude toward it, with him because he sees her as an ideal woman.

Another poem of the same year, "Une Allée du Luxembourg," shows again the influence of Ronsard. A simple, straightforward poem, it consists of three stanzas of four octosyllabic lines. The poet relates that he has seen a girl, carrying a flower and humming a new melody, pass quickly by. The stanza is purely descriptive. The personal element enters in the second stanza where the poet says that she "is perhaps the only one in the world whose heart would respond to (his), who entering (his) profound darkness would illuminate it with a single glance."[18] The idea opens the realm of possibility to the poet, but the possibility has already been negated because "She has passed by."[19] The use of the conditional tense adds to the poignancy of an impossible relationship—poignant because of the use of the superlative adjective *seule* twice even though she is the only one who can alleviate the poet's melancholy. A definite negation appears in the third stanza. "No, my youth is over. Farewell, gentle ray that shone on me,—Perfume, girl, harmony . . . Happiness was passing by. It fled."[20] The use of the verb tenses, the punctuation, and the repetition of the flower, girl, and music of the first stanza indicate the melancholy tone of the poem and give it its unity. We know from the first line that the girl has passed by—a completed action. The use of the conditional tense in the second stanza relates what might have happened. In the third there is the definite assertion in the present, "My youth is over," but it implies the past. "Happiness was passing by . . ." in the imperfect tense seems to imply again that it might have stopped for him, but this possibility is negated by the simple and powerful "It fled." The seemingly bizarre use of punctuation, which is a peculiarity of Nerval's style, is found especially in the third stanza with its use of three dashes as well as three dots after the first and third lines. These punctuational devices tend to break the rhythm of the stanza and demonstrate the poet's confusion in his sad state. It is not just the confusion, however, it is the pain that he is experiencing that is augmented

by the use of the four rhymes with the sound "i." Technically,
the poem seems simple, but the use of the accents shows Nerval
to be an extremely proficient craftsman. *Elle a passé, la jeune fille*
is accented on the fourth and eighth syllables as is the second
line, *Vive et preste comme un oiseau*; but in lines three and four,
A la main une fleur qui brille, / A la bouche un refrain nouveau,
the accents are on the third, sixth, and eighth syllables. This
makes not only for metrical variety, but shows a developing
musicality from first to fourth line, where the description itself
is more lyrical. In the second stanza, line one is accented on the
fourth and eighth syllables, line two on the third, fifth, and
eighth, line three on the third, sixth, and eighth, and line four
on the fourth and eighth. There is already a slight breakdown
in the rhythm due to the different irregular accents of the middle
lines. This breakdown, paralleling the poet's unhappiness, is
fully shown in the third stanza with its punctuational pauses
and breaks. The tension of the poem comes from the contrast
between the sense of melancholy and the basic lyric quality
of the poem.

Four other poems were written by Nerval in 1832: "Nobles
et valets," "Le Reveil en voiture," "Le Relais," and "Notre
Dame de Paris." None is a great poem, although each is of more
than passing interest. "Nobles et valets" is a satirical poem
which contrasts the virtues of the nobility of the past with the
faults of that social group in the present. The tone of the poem
is ironic for Nerval is attacking the nobility of the 1830's as a
race of "Larridons." Larridon is the name of a dog in a fable
by La Fontaine. He was always hanging around the kitchen
waiting for handouts, just as these nobles hang around the
ministries, "groveling, greedy, and degraded."[21] They wear
corsets, shirt fronts, and calf padding. The satire is harsh and,
although effective, rather uncharacteristic of the poet. There is
also an implicit snobbishness on Nerval's part, for the title refers
to the daughters of the old nobility who have mingled their blood
with that of the valets to give rise to this new race of Larridons.

"Le Reveil en voiture," a three-stanza poem in alexandrines,
is of interest because of the pre-Fauvist picture it paints of the
nature perceived by the poet in the process of awakening in
a carriage. By means of verbal comparisons and rhythmic

enjambements Nerval evokes an unbalanced and quickly moving landscape. The poem's basic weakness is found in its final line: "I was traveling past and just awakening,"[22] which, in its very explicitness lessens the suggestive quality of the rest of the poem. The title alone provides the key to the poem, and there seems little need for it to be reemphasized in the final line.

"Le Relais" is an occasional piece, a banal description of what one does while waiting for horses to be changed. Technically and descriptively it is inferior to any other poem Nerval wrote during this period. "Notre-Dame de Paris" is a better poem. Its theme is that when Notre-Dame has fallen into ruins, people from all over the world will come to see it because they have read Victor Hugo's book which will recreate it completely for them. The first two lines are basically prosaic: "Notre-Dame is quite old. One will, however, perhaps see it bury Paris which it saw being born."[23] The next four lines contain a powerful image. "But in several thousand years, as a wolf an ox, time will make this heavy carcass budge, will twist its iron nerves, and then with a dull tooth will sadly gnaw its old bones of stone."[24] The use of the word "sadly" hurts the image for time has no emotions, and its use is therefore a bad example of the pathetic fallacy. Actually, the comment is being made by the poet, the entrance of whose feelings into the poem is unnecessary at this point.

A characteristic of the poem is the use of indefinites—"quite old," "perhaps," "however some thousand years," "many men." In certain lines these words seem to be padding used to fill out the metrical requirements. The major verb tense in the poem is the future which, because of adverbial qualifiers, implies indefiniteness in the first stanza and definiteness in the second:

Many men from every country in the world will come to contemplate this austere ruin—dreamers rereading Victor's book. Then they will believe they have seen the old basilica just as it was—powerful and magnificent, rise up before them like the shadow of the dead.[25]

As poetry of homage, "Notre-Dame de Paris" is a respectable poem, but it cannot match the great poems of the same year— "Avril" and "Fantaisie."

It was not until 1835 that another poem of Nerval was published, and only two, "La Grand'mère" and "Dans les bois," were published then. "La Grand'mère," actually written in 1831, three years after his grandmother's death, is of interest for the insight it gives into Nerval's personality. The poem is concerned with the durability of memory. Like Meursault, Nerval tells us that he did not weep or lament at his grandmother's funeral, and he was reproached for his seeming lack of feeling. But those who wept with true and bitter grief before have now, because of the business of living, forgotten her. The poet, however, has not forgotten: "I alone think of her and often weep for her; for three years, growing stronger with time like a name carved in the bark of a tree her memory comes to the fore."[26] The tone of the poem, which is both narrative and descriptive, is simple and familial, and in its very simplicity lies its naive charm. But most important is the insight the poem gives into Nerval's psychology. For him, even at the age of twenty-three, past emotion is always alive and tends, through memory, to increase with the passage of time. The power of the past, suggested in "La Grand'mère," will develop, as Nerval matures, into a full-fledged mythology in which the dead are as alive, if not more so, as the living, and Nerval, as he describes in *Aurélia,* falls more and more under their spell.

"Dans les bois," reminiscent of Ronsard's shorter works, is another implicitly personal poem of much lyric charm. The language is simple, and the octosyllabic lines with their *rimes croisées* have a melodious flow. The repetition of the haunting phrase, *dans les bois* (in the woods), at the end of each stanza unifies the poem and describes as well the world of nature which has its own laws of instinct. This is a world to which Nerval, by implication, unfavorably compares man and especially himself. The bird is born and sings in the spring. In summer it seeks a mate and "loves, loves only once. How gentle, peaceful, and faithful the bird's nest is. . . ."[27] In autumn the bird no longer sings and soon dies fulfilling nature's plan. The last two lines show the relationship of the poet to the poem: "Alas, how happy the death of the bird must be—in the woods."[28] The poet envies the bird his song, his love, and even his death which he sees as happy because the bird has experienced the purest forms of life. Nerval seeks most the happy, peaceful, faithful love of the bird, a love which we know from his biography and works he himself never found.

"De Ramsgate à Anvers," written in June, 1837, and published in 1846, is one of Nerval's longest poems. It contains fifteen stanzas of six-syllable-line quatrains with *rimes croisées*. The descriptive parts of the poem do not really paint a visual picture; instead, the poet presents abstractions or occasionally clichés. (Nerval never was, even in his prose writings, the natural colorist that so many of his contemporaries in all the arts were.) A typical example is, "I therefore said good-bye to the English coast, and its white cliffs are disappearing on the horizon."[29] Most of the poem, however, is a tribute to Rubens, the great Antwerp painter. Unlike Baudelaire in "Les Phares," Nerval does not comment on the sensuality in Rubens's paintings but thinks more of them in terms of richness of texture and mythological subject matter. (Nerval claims Rubens is "cold to realities.") He writes of the Marie de Medici paintings in the Louvre, but mistakes her for Catherine de Medici who married the Valois king Henri II. Some of Nerval's descriptions of the paintings are excellent, but it is apparent that, unlike Baudelaire, he is seeing the subject matter and surfaces rather than the mind that created the paintings. Here again is seen Nerval's obsession with the past, and especially with the Valois. The typical romantic concept of genius is also evinced in "De Ramsgate à Anvers": "Joy, love, and delirium, alas, expiated too much! The kings on the ship and the gods at their feet!—Farewell, ended splendor of a solemn century! But you alone, o genius! you remain eternal."[30]

"A M. Alexandre Dumas à Francfort" is an amusing occasional poem describing Nerval's financial difficulties on his way to meet Dumas in Frankfort. Its demonstration of Nerval's wit occasioned Dumas to write of it: "This versified note in the taste of Louis XIII . . . gives evidence I believe of some philosophy. . . ."[31] The poem, written in 1838, was published by Dumas in 1854.

"Résignation" (1839, published 1897) is a ten-stanza poem written in quatrains of three alexandrines and one six-syllable line with *rimes croisées*. This is the last dated poem before Nerval's breakdown in 1841, and it expresses a sadness that the poet finds insuperable. As in many other of his early poems, the descriptions of nature are in pastel hues rather than highly colored, and they resemble more the poetry of the eighteenth century than of his own:

When the first fires of the sun inundate nature, when all shines in my eyes with life and love; if I see a flower, fresh and pure, open to the rays of a lovely day; if joyous flocks bound about the plain, if the bird sings in the woods where I'm going to wander, I'm sad and feel my soul so full of mourning that I should like to weep.[32]

The "fires of the sun" is a cliché, and the description is generalized: no object is distinguished by a novel descriptive phrase. The flower is "fresh and pure," the flocks "joyous," the bird sings, the sun shines. None of the highly colored and often original imagery we associate with Romanticism is found here. Nerval is rather interested in the mood this monochromatic landscape of happiness evokes in him. If he sees the beauties of nature, if he hears the bird's song, he is sad. But he writes:

But when I see the grass of the meadow dry up, when the leaf of the woods falls yellow at my feet, when I see a pale sky or a withered rose, I sit down dreaming. And I feel less sad, and my hand picks up these leaves, this débris of greenness and flowers. I like to look at them; my mouth kisses them . . . I say to them, "O my sisters!"[33]

It is not therefore painting of the external world that concerns Nerval, but rather the effect of this world on his own sensibilities. In "Résignation" Nerval identifies with dissolution and decay and asks in a premonitory way, "Am I not going to descend into the tomb in my springtime days?"[34]—a thought that recurs throughout much of his work. More interesting, however, is the following stanza: "Perhaps, like me, this dying flower opening with joy to the ardors of the sun enclosed in its breast the devouring flame that killed it."[35] The obsession with sun and fire that appears throughout the poet's works is important to note, for the idea that he harbors within himself the seeds of his own destruction implies his sense of guilt, a sense that will overwhelm his mind in later years.

"Résignation" is basically a meditation à la Lamartine. Even much of the language and rhythm is Lamartinian as, in the seventh stanza which follows the one quoted above, he writes: "Necessity has it that here below everything fades, all passes. Why fear a fate that each must undergo? Death is only a sleep. Since my soul is tired let it go to sleep."[36] Immediately following this is the exclamation "My mother!... Oh, out of pity since I must die, friends, spare her unnecessary grief. Soon she will come towards my sad dwelling, but I shall not be there."[37] The stanza is confusing because Nerval's mother had died when he was an infant. One wonders momentarily if he has resurrected the dead and lost his rationality. His sad dwelling would seem to be his tomb, but if he is not there, where is he? The answer is found in the last two stanzas:

And you, adored dream of my solitary heart, beautiful and laughing child whom I loved hopelessly, your memory attaches me to the earth in vain. I must no longer see you. But if for a long time my ghost, like a vain image, appears to you ... oh! don't be afraid, for my ghost will follow you for a long time, uncertain between heaven and you.[38]

The poem then has been caused by a hopeless love to which the poet has become resigned and because of which he will die. But despite its rather banal language Nerval is not striking a typical Romantic pose. The eighth stanza with its apostrophe to his mother is heartfelt and shows that his mind is confused. It would appear that life after death is a necessity for Nerval, for without it there is nothing, no goal, no possible happiness. This is the reason for his seeing his mother as being alive and he himself after death living for his beloved. The question that is raised is, which is to be more wished for—heaven or her? "Résignation" is certainly a prelude to the delusions and manic concepts described in *Aurélia*. It appears from all the poetry written before the first certified mental crisis of 1841 that the seeds of that crisis are already in evidence.

The first poem that we know to have been written after Nerval's first spell of madness is one addressed to Victor Hugo thanking him for a gift of his book *Le Rhin*. Like the earlier "Notre Dame de Paris," it is a poem of homage. The poem was not published until the 1950's, and on the other side of the manuscript are some lines addressed to one Eugénie whose identity is in doubt.

> O mother of the unfortunate
> Pity all those who are abandoned.
> Be happy and pardon
> If you wish God to pardon.[39]

The myth of the mother-lover-goddess is already apparent in this quatrain, and she becomes a dominant figure in Nerval's works after 1841.

II *New Paths*

The earliest of the *Chimères* for which we have a date is "Delfica," first written under the title of "Vers dorés" and dated Tivoli, 1843. It was published on December 28, 1845, eight months after the publication of the poem now called "Vers dorés" on the sixteenth of March, under the title "Pensée antique." Not only is "Delfica" the first of Nerval's sonnets of which we have a record, but it marks a complete break with his previous styles of writing as well as with their content.

Delfica evokes Delphi, the shrine of Apollo, god of poetry. Daphne, a nymph beloved of him, rejected his advances and was turned into a laurel tree. In the first quatrain Nerval familiarly asks her an obviously rhetorical question, "Daphne, do you know that ancient romance, that song of love that is always renewed at the foot of the sycamore or under the white laurels, under the olive tree, the myrtle or trembling willow?..."[40] The poet's syncretism is evident in this verse for the sycamore is a Christian symbol. The Holy Family is supposed to have rested under one on their flight to Egypt. The olive is sacred to Athena, the myrtle to Aphrodite, the laurel to Apollo (white indicates Daphne's purity), and the willow is a symbol of death. In this first quatrain ancient Greece is evoked, but so are its links to the present. The story of Apollo and Daphne had parallels in Nerval's own personal life. He, the poet, pursued his "goddesses" and ultimately was rebuffed by them. He therefore sees them as unobtainable and thus as pure objects of love and veneration. They were as inaccessible to him in human physical terms as the Daphne-turned-laurel was to Apollo. The *ancienne romance* transcends chronological time and takes on a mystical aspect that combines elements of intellect, poetry, fire, love, beauty, Christian charity, purity, and *agape*.

In the second quatrain, the poet asks Daphne if she recognizes "the Temple with the immense peristyle."[41] The capitalized T in Temple indicates a certain temple or perhaps the idea of a temple in general. One first thinks of the Temple of Apollo at Delphi, but the next lines, "(Do you recognize) the bitter lemons into which your teeth bit and the grotto, fatal to imprudent guests, where the ancient seeds of the conquered dragon sleep . . . ,"[42] indicate a change of scene and give evidence of the mingling of personal memories, ancient mythologies, and literary references into a new mythology. Elements of the Delphic story are found in the Temple (it was *the* temple of ancient Greece), and the killing of the dragon (python) by the child Apollo (the Temple of Delphi with its famed Pythian priestess stood on the spot where the killing occurred). There is a reference as well to Cadmus, who went to Delphi for advice on how to find his aunt Europa. He was told to settle on the spot where a cow he would find on leaving the temple lay down. He was led by her to Thebes which he settled. To get water, he killed a dragon which was guarding the source. Punished by Ares for the murder of his offspring, Cadmus was told by Athena to sow the dragon's teeth. He did so and there appeared a harvest of armed men whom he killed by setting them to fight one another. Five survived and became the ancestors of the royalty of Thebes and Sparta.[43]

Another mythological reference is to the grotto of the Sirens whose irresistible song lured sailors to their death. Since the grotto is at Capri, the famous Temple of Isis at Pompeii is brought to mind, and it is possible that Nerval is syncretically associating it with the Temple of Apollo. Combined with these classical images are personal references and recollections of his readings. His translation of Part II of Goethe's *Faust* in 1840 was accompanied by a translation of Mignon's song "Kennst du das Land?" One stanza reads:

Do you know the country where in the dark foliage the fruit of the lemon tree shines like a fruit of gold, where the wind of a blue sky refreshes without storm the bowers of myrtle and woods of laurel? . . .

Do you know the house, the wide peristyle, and the somber cavern
where the old serpent sleeps?[44]

Mignon, away from her beloved Italy, sings longingly of it.
Daphne, too, may well represent a girl Nerval knew in Italy
and of whom he speaks in "El Desdichado" and *Octavie*. Thus,
a major characteristic of Nerval's later poetry becomes evident:
His mythologies and memories unite into a single world.

The second quatrain has ominous overtones. At the caesuras
of the final three lines, the words "bitter," "fatal," and "conquered" are emphasized. A sense of loss is suggested, but the
loss is not irreparable—the seeds of the dragon are only asleep.
The question posed is whether there will be a new harvest or
perhaps a revival of the values and beauties of antiquity.

The first tercet answers the question, "Those gods for whom
you weep will return. Time will bring back the order of
the ancient days. The earth has trembled with a prophetic
breath. . . ."[45] The ambivalence of the woman addressed adds
new overtones to the poem. Both the mythological Daphne in
her arboreal prison and the modern one in her various guises
(Octavie, Mignon) will see a new order, yet one that is ancient.
Time will again become one—past and present unified. This
is harbingered by the possibility of Vesuvius erupting. The
landscape, which until now has been suggested as Greek, has
subtly become Italian. From Delphi the poet has moved to
Naples and its environs with Vesuvius, the Temple of Isis
Nerval saw near there, the memory of Vergil's laurel, the gate-
way to the Inferno through which the Latin poet led Dante,
the reference to the poem's having been written in Tivoli, the
flora—lemon trees common to the region, and his own memories
of a happy sojourn there, a time now past. An age of gold, of
perfect love, a past time that is really a unity with the present—
all will return. The three dots at the end of the tercet imply a
pause and suggest a questioning of his assumption which is
brought out in the last tercet, which begins with the word
"However." "However, the Sibyl with the Latin face is still
sleeping under the Arch of Constantine—and nothing has disturbed the severe portico."[46] The movement is from possibility
to near-negation, but the door is not really closed. The Cumaean

Sibyl, who, like the Pythian priestess, foretold the future, is still
sleeping beneath a symbol of the end of paganism and triumph
of Christianity under Constantine. Sleeping implies awaking,
and the "romance" which always begins again will be heard
once more. The poet, however, does not know when or how,
and this lack of knowledge gives the poem its slightly pessimistic tone.

In "Delfica" many of the characteristics of Nerval's later
masterpieces are found. The combination of specific references
(mythology, geography, literary allusions) with suggestive references (memories of the poet's personal life, the ambiguity of
the identity of Daphne), the blending of different cultures
(Greek, Roman, modern) into what might become (and does
in his later works) a new mythology give "Delfica" a quality
both musical (suggested) and marmoreal (stated). The combination of these two aspects gives the sonnet its haunting and
original quality. The quatrains contain the music, the tercets the
marmoreal aspects. The sonnet is one of movement. Words like
"recommence," "recognize," "return," "bring back" give the
impression of perpetual movement and suggest cycles of time.
But time is never dead. It is always one, always present; even
if the past seems to be dead or sleeping, it is still alive. "Delfica"
is a poem of time—time mythologized, time remembered, time
foreseen. All coexists in time—love, history, poetry, religion. The
richness of the allusions, the suggestive references, the choice of
nasal sounds to lengthen the lines and give them their stately
music are new elements in Nerval's poetry, and the combination
is unique in this period of French Romanticism.

The next dated poem from the *Chimères* is "Christ aux
oliviers," a poem consisting of five sonnets published in March,
1844, and inspired by a poem of Jean Paul Richter—"Discours
du Christ mort"—in which the German poet expresses his horror
of nothingness in a godless universe. Vigny's poem "Le Mont
des oliviers" was published three months later than Nerval's
and seems also to have been inspired by Richter's poem.

These five sonnets differ greatly from "Delfica." Their references are more readily available to the reader; they form a
narrative sequence; the philosophy is less arcane, and it is a
less personal and more humanistic poem. Christ on the Mount

of Olives raises his thin arms to heaven. He is in a state of
anguish and feels Himself betrayed by ungrateful friends. Below,
His disciples, dreaming of future honors, sleep, but their sleep
is that "of animals."[47] They are unaware of their Master's agony.
Christ turns to them and cries "God does not exist," but they
continue to sleep. The repetition of the phrase *ils dormaient*
("they kept on sleeping") shows their indifference to Christ's
problems and points up the tragic aspects of His isolation.
Although He has no listeners, Christ continues to speak. He
relates that He has "touched the eternal vault of heaven with
His forehead" and has been "bloody, broken, suffering for
many days."[48] (Nerval's use of the line *Je suis sanglant, brisé,
souffrant pour bien des jours* with its accents on, and pauses
after, the fourth, sixth, eighth and twelfth syllables gives it a
length that well expresses the suffering of Christ.) He claims
He has deceived His disciples. "There is no God at the altar
where I am the victim. God is not. God is no longer."[49]

In the second and most descriptive sonnet of the series, Christ
recounts His search for God in the universe, but He is notably
absent. The third sonnet (which, along with the second, owes the
most to Richter) continues the monologue of Christ, and the
language used is almost a translation of the German poem:

Immobile Destiny, mute sentinel, Cold Necessity! . . . Chance which,
preceding you among the worlds dead under eternal snow, frozen
by degrees, the universe paling, do you know what you're doing,
original power, with your extinguished suns, each brushing past the
other. . . . Are you sure of transmitting an immortal breath between
a dying world and the other being born?[50]

Christ is questioning Chance and wondering if the dying world
is the pagan one, Christianity the one being born. He then asks
God (who He claims no longer exists if it is He whom Christ
feels in Himself) if He has the power of life and conquering
death or has He succumbed to Satan's power. Christ feels alone
in His suffering, and if He dies all will die.

The fourth and fifth sonnets are written more in the less
rhetorical style of the later Nerval. The fourth shows human
indifference to His plight and continues the narration of the
first sonnet:

None heard the eternal victim moan. Giving His whole overflowing heart up to the world in vain, but ready to faint and strengthless, leaning over, He called the *only one* awake in Jerusalem. "Judas," He cried to him, "hasten to sell Me and finish this transaction. Friend, I'm suffering and lying on the earth. Come, o you who at least have the strength of crime!"[51]

Christ knows that Judas has his role to play and is anxious for it to be enacted, but the betrayer is not happy with this role because he knows that it is one for which he will be damned for eternity. Pilate, Caesar's emissary, feeling some pity, tells his underlings to seek out "this madman."[52]

In the fifth sonnet, a crucial aspect of Nerval's beliefs is found. Christ, "this sublime madman," is identified with others who had attempted the impossible: Icarus, who tried to fly; Phaeton, who stole Apollo's chariot and was burned to death by the sun; Atys, a fertility figure and lover of Cybele. Nerval's religious syncretism is demonstrated as he shows elements common to all religions and evokes a single belief which attests to mankind's eternal aspirations:

The soothsayer questioned the flank of the victim; the earth became drunk on this precious blood. The stunned universe tilted on its axles, and Olympus, for an instant, staggered towards the abyss. "Answer," cried Caesar to Jupiter Ammon. "What is this new god who is imposed on the earth? And if he's not a god he's at least a demon." But the invoked oracle had to be silent forever. Only one could explain this mystery to the world: He who gave birth to the children of the earth.[53]

Yet He is dead, and there apparently can be no solution. Nerval here hints at the enmity, later to be discussed and developed in *Aurélia*, between the children of the earth, descendants of Adam, and the children of fire, descendants of Cain and adversaries of the Judeo-Christian God. Nerval often identifies with the latter children, yet in this poem he does experience compassion for the anguished Christ.

The sonnets are of unequal value. The first, fourth, and fifth, the three regular sonnets, show Nerval's mastery of irony and evocative allusions. The third has a majesty in its philosophical questioning that is worthy of Vigny, but Nerval's Christ lacks the cold and philosophical disdain of Vigny's. He is much more human, even if he is less interested in human suffering. His sense of loneliness, his fear of a meaningless death renders Christ a tragic figure Who remains essentially human. The unequal value of the sonnets and the often bizarre turns of phrase within them make "Le Christ aux oliviers" less effective, if more accessible, than the other sonnets of *Les Chimères*, but at its best it shows Nerval to be a great poet.

"Vers dorés," another of the *Chimères*, was published in 1845 under the title "Pensée antique." There are reminiscences of Hugo's pantheistic views in this poem, and it is a forerunner of Baudelaire's theory of correspondences. Pythagorean in tone, the poem is preceded by a citation from Pythagoras which relates that everything has feeling.[54] Nerval's theories of metempsychosis were influenced by what he knew of the Orphic mysteries as well as Vergil's *Fourth Eclogue*. The poet believes that soul exists in all living matter, that man can be distinguished from the vegetable and animal worlds only by his power of acting and choosing freely.

The sonnet begins in a tone of scorn, and then the tone changes to one of instruction:

Man, freethinker!, do you believe yourself the only thinking being in this world where life bursts forth in everything? Your freedom disposes of the forces you hold, but from all your councils the universe is absent. Respect in the animal an active spirit; Each flower is a soul blossoming in Nature; A mystery of love reposes in the mineral. "Everything has feeling!" And everything has power over your being. Fear in the blind wall a look that spies on you: a voice is attached to matter itself ... Don't make it serve an impious use! Often a hidden God inhabits the humble being; and like a new-born eye covered by its lids a pure spirit is growing under the bark of stones.[55]

"Vers dorés" is the poem of a seer who perceives mysterious correspondences in a universal harmony. Man, blinded either by ignorance or his own sense of self-importance, may be unaware of the powers of the universe and thus lack a sense of awe before the miracle of the creation and a knowledge of his place in it. Man should see beyond appearances and venerate Nature, for a hidden God may be found where least expected, and a new aspect of the universe perceived. Nerval is suggesting that man should increase his perceptive horizons as he, the poet, has done and thus become a conscious part of a perfect, though mysterious, world.

The role of man in nature is a favorite theme of the Romantic poets, and "Vers dorés" has much in common both in subject and in imagery, especially the image of the eye, with Hugo's "A Albert Durer" and Baudelaire's "Correspondances." In this poem Nerval is the Romantic mystic rather than the possessed mystic of *Aurélia* and certain of the *Chimères*, but, needless to say, this does not affect the beauty or sense of ecstasy found in the poem, one of the most accessible of Nerval's sonnets.

Nerval in 1845 was still capable, however, of writing banal and embarrassingly bad poetry. In this year, as well as "Vers dorés," he wrote "Une Femme est l'amour," a three-stanza poem of quatrains in alexandrines. Here he glorifies the housewife as love, *gloire,* and hope. She is like a "heavenly spirit exiled on earth."[56] The poem might well have had appeal to the bourgeois of Nerval's time, but, except for the deification of woman (here even the ordinary housewife), it is one of the worst and least characteristic of his poems.

"Rêverie de Charles VI," written in 1842 but published in 1847 and subtitled "Fragment," is one of Nerval's key poems. Written basically in alexandrine couplets, the poem is irregular because neither the first nor the fourth lines have rhymes, and there are three dots before the first line implying that other lines may have been present at one time, lines that Nerval chose, perhaps, not to publish.

Charles VI (1368–1422) was a significant choice of subject for the poet. Attaining the throne at the age of twelve, Charles later became excessive in his living habits, and in 1392 he had an attack of madness at Le Mans. Other attacks followed and, although still nominally king, he lost his power and spent the rest of his life in a state of neglect at Senlis. Since the poem was originally written in 1842, after Nerval's first major attack of madness, certain parallels between the poet and the king exist, parallels of which Nerval must have been aware. It is quite possible then to discuss this poem as being spoken by Gérard as the double of Charles rather than by Charles VI himself.

The pessimism of the poem gives a strong indication of Nerval's state of mind when he wrote it. Charles bewails his throne and asks why God "still puts this painful burden on (his) head which is abandoned to sad thoughts and suffering and already bowed by itself."[57] Charles would have preferred a calm and obscure life in nature. He says:

Oh, those vermillion, capricious flames of the sunset rise like a splendid road towards the heavens! It seems that God is saying to my suffering soul, "Leave the impure world, the indifferent crowd; follow with a *steady* step this shining road, and—come to me, my son . . . and—don't wait for THE NIGHT! ! !"[58]

On the manuscript over the word "night" are the number fifty-two and a T-shaped cross. The meaning of fifty-two is obscure, but a T-shaped cross symbolically emphasizes the near equilibrium of the opposing principles of the spiritual world and the world of phenomena. It could thus be a symbol of agony, struggle, martyrdom. The quotation cited above suggests suicide, for the night is often associated by Nerval with madness, and this state can lead to death. The italicization of "steady" indicates the importance of the fact that there is to be no faltering. The circumstances under which this poem was written and the reason for its publication five years later are not known, but there is a strong indication that Nerval, having just recovered from a state of madness, was contemplating suicide.

As a poem, "Rêverie de Charles VI" is a fragment, and its literary value is small, although certain lines have a remarkable authority and rhythm. But most of the poem deals with the kind of life Charles would like to have had, the rustic life idealized by many Romantic poets. The language in this section is neither original nor striking. It functions at best to set off the beginning and end of the poem. Yet the poem has its hermetic elements that are of interest, and as a psychological portrait of a desperate man "Rêverie de Charles VI" has remarkable power.

"L'Abbaye Saint-Germain-des-Prés" (1847) is a tribute to the painter Gigoux. The two-stanza eight-line poem in alexandrines is irregular because the final two lines do not rhyme (*gloire*/*élève*). The interest of this short piece is Nerval's comment that genius has its rights, and even worldly power must pay homage to it.

Many of the poems published between 1852 and 1854 may, in some cases must, have been written earlier, but their first appearance in print was in the *Petits Châteaux de Bohème* or *Les Filles du feu.* Among these poems are "La Cousine," an odelette that must have pleased the public because of its familiar tone and clean outdoors atmosphere. It depicts the pleasures of Nerval and a cousin in the Tuileries, and then the return home to a fine turkey dinner. "Gaieté," another odelette, is a wry poem, full of charm and piquancy. It is a paean to wine in the style of Ronsard, and ends on an amusing note as the poet says he cannot find a word to rhyme with *pampre.* Personal, lighthearted, "Gaieté," like "La Cousine," seems to have been written in the early 1830's because it is closer in tone and language to the poetry Nerval wrote during that period. Another odelette, "Les Cydalises," is a reminiscence of Gérard's bohemian days which are described in *Petits Châteaux de Bohème.* The Cydalises were the girls who frequented the apartment Nerval shared with several artist friends, but the poem is sad for the girls are no longer alive. "Where are our girls? They're in the tomb. They're happier in a more beautiful land."[59] There is not much originality technically or linguistically, but the poem is another statement of Nerval's myth of the assumption of love by death.

"Madame et Souveraine" (1852) and "Epitaphe" were both written in a letter to Madame de Solms, a nineteen-year-old Napoleonic princess. The former begins with a quotation from Chérubin's song from Beaumarchais's *Le Mariage de Figaro,* "Madame and Sovereign, how troubled is my heart...."[60] Chérubin sings the song to the Countess Almaviva with whom he is in love. Nerval claims that this refrain has wandered through his brain all night and left him sad. He relates in the poem that he is full of regrets for his life:

I am a lazy bohemian journalist who dines on witticism spread out on his bread. Old before his time and full of bitter rancor, distrustful as a rat, deceived by too many people, not believing at all in sincere friendship . . .[61]

The depression that fills these lines is poignant, and he continues to give a description of his pathetic abode and way of life, for at this time Nerval was a victim of poverty. He relates that he cannot write in winter because his pen is frozen and he is "without heat in his hovel, without panes in his windows."[62] He is going to find "The *way* to heaven or hell and has fastened (his) gaiters for the other world."[63] He continues:

I have written my epitaph and take the liberty to dedicate it to you in a stupid sonnet which bursts forth right now from the depths of an empty brain . . . the movement of a cuckoo stopped by the cold. Misery has made my thought null and void.[64]

Certainly Nerval's circumstances were wretched at this period in his life, and the threat of death, by which he had always been obsessed, in the form of suicide is omnipresent. Written as an epistle with moments of what we today might call black humor, "Madame et Souveraine" indicates the fragile state of mind and body of the poet at the end of 1852.

"Epitaphe" is, as Nerval has mentioned, a sonnet pessimistic in tone, written in a spirit of futility, expressing a sense of depression about the uselessness of his life. Although formally a sonnet, "Epitaphe" has many characteristics of a narrative ballad:

He lived gaily at times like a starling, in turn a careless or tender lover, at times somber and dreamy like a sad Clitandre. One day he heard someone knocking at his door.
It was Death! So he asked her to wait until he had put the finishing touch to his last sonnet. And then, without becoming excited, he lay down in the bottom of the cold coffin where his body shivered. He was lazy, according to stories; he let the ink in his inkwell dry up too much; he wanted to know all, but knew nothing. And when, tired of this life, the moment of death came one winter's night he went off saying, "Why did I come?"[65]

The fear of creative sterility, the lack of artistic discipline, the Faustian desire to have complete knowledge had all haunted him throughout his life, and his awareness of his failure was complete. Today, however, although his output of masterpieces was small, we find his creative life a success.

III Summa

Les Chimères was originally published as a pendant to *Les Filles du feu* in 1854. Some, including "Delfica," "Vers dorés," and "Le Christ aux oliviers," had been published in the eighteen forties. When the others were written is not known, but many of them would seem to have been written after 1851. The title *Chimères,* with its suggestive overtones, is a word used often by Nerval, but its most interesting and pertinent use is found in an essay Nerval wrote on Heine's *Intermezzo*: "Woman is the chimera of man or his demon, as you will—an adorable monster, but a monster."[66] Woman is one of the causes of unity in *Les Chimères.* In all the sonnets but the final two ("Le Christ aux oliviers" and "Vers dorés"), woman—real, mythological, religious—plays a most important role in the mind of the poet and becomes, as in *Aurélia,* transformed into *the* woman, unobtainable, cause of exaltation and despair, becoming, in short, an all-powerful goddess. All the poems deal as well with time and the unity of past, present, and future, time of memory, man-created time, universal time, mythological time. It might be said that these sonnets represent the victory over time by Nerval, for time obsessed him as much as it did Proust sixty years later.

Only poetry with its suggestibility could really encompass the whole of Nerval's thought. His memories, his readings, his religious aspirations, his personal mythology are found intertwined in this group of poems. The sonnet form in essence is quite restrictive, but Nerval, now the master, extends its limitations. These sonnets contain ideas and symbols which, in their hermetic density, constantly fight against the imposed form, and from this struggle come the tension and beauty of the poems. Because of their hermetic quality it is often, if not always, difficult to discuss these poems as deeply as one might wish. Each time one reads a line, a quatrain, a tercet, or the complete sonnet, new reverberations of meaning appear, echoes calling up echoes when the original sound is lost. Yet it is possible to discuss each of the poems in such a way as to indicate to the reader its subject, many of its allusions, and the technique used by Nerval to express his thoughts. These sonnets, with *Aurélia,* represent the *summa* of Nerval's art and thought, for in them is to be found everything that intrigued, haunted, or obsessed him throughout his career. Nerval himself, in his dedication to *Les Filles du feu,* writes to Alexandre Dumas:

And since you had the imprudence to cite one of the sonnets composed in that state of *super-naturalist* reverie, as the Germans say, you must hear them all. —You will find them at the end of the volume. They are scarcely less obscure than the metaphysics of Hegel or the *Memorabilia* of Swedenborg, and they would lose their charm by being explained, if the thing were possible. Grant me at least the merit of the expression.[67]

These comments explain why the poems are hermetic. Nerval implies that they might be explained (much as Rimbaud later claimed that he alone had the key to "Parade") but by elucidating them they might lose much of their suggestive power. Yet it is possible to explain aspects of them so that the reader who is not acquainted with Nerval will have at least some insights into the poems and then on his own discover their great beauty.

"El Desdichado" is the first sonnet of *Les Chimères* and the best known. Rightly so, moreover, for it is one of the greatest poems in French literature. Nerval took his title—the Disinherited One—from the eighth chapter of Sir Walter Scott's *Ivanhoe,* where it is the motto of one of the knights. Although another title, "Le Destin," is found on one of the manuscripts that belonged to Paul Eluard, the title of the printed version is more apt because the sonnet is one of the most personal poems of the author, and it describes more accurately the sonnet's contents.

The first line of the sonnet is ominous, "I am the man of shadows,—the widower,—the inconsolable one."[68] The untraditional pauses between adjectives or nouns used adjectively lengthen the alexandrine and give it a dislocated quality which well describes the poet's state of mind. The progression from "man of shadows" to "the inconsolable one" evinces an ascending order of intensity as well as of hopelessness. The "man of shadows" is not necessarily a superlative, but "widower" and "inconsolable one" are. Yet all three are preceded by the article "the" which gives them a fixed, unchangeable quality, and the line, thus, becomes a statement of unrelieved desperation.

The second line, "The Prince of Acquitaine in the destroyed tower," continues the air of hopelessness. The reference to the Prince is vague, for there were many Aquitanian princes (and Nerval often identified with royalty), but the line suggests again exile, desperation, and homelessness. The reason for this state is given next, "My only *star* is dead,—and my constellated lute bears the black *sun* of Melancholy." The poet is a widower and inconsolable because his "star" (his beloved) is dead, and his empyreal lute (or muse) mourns the deceased. The black sun of melancholy is used almost as an heraldic term, a symbol of loss, despair, and inability, even through poetry, to find salvation. The engraving of *Melancholia* by Dürer was known to Nerval (as well as to many of his contemporaries who, like Hugo and Baudelaire, made use of it in their works), for a reproduction of it appeared at the head of the first number of a review, *Le Carrousel* (1836), which contained an article praising Jenny Colon. This engraving, found again in *Aurélia*, unconsciously, perhaps, became the symbol of Nerval's dead love.

Because of the poet's knowledge of, and interest in, all forms of mysticism, it is possible to see in this quatrain the influence of the Tarot cards. The sixteenth card of the Major Arcana— the Lightning-struck Tower, or, as it is called in France, La Maison Dieu—signifies the fall of the Angels or the fall from both physical and spiritual grace. It is probably linked in Nerval's mind with the Cainites, the children of fire (fire is lashing the upper section of the crumbling tower) with whom he identified. The seventeenth card is the Star, which depicts a naked woman emptying two pitchers. This card represents wisdom, spiritual intelligence, hope, happiness. It is also the symbol of speech. The star to which Nerval refers could then be the cause of the loss of his communicative ability as well as his hope and happiness which would be in keeping with the tone of the quatrain. But for Nerval, as for Dante, the star also represents the inaccessible purity of the beloved (as in *Sylvie* and *Aurélia*), but in "El Desdichado" the star is dead; The object of veneration has deserted the poet and caused his complete despair. The nineteenth Tarot card is the Sun, the life-giving force, but read in conjunction with the Lightning-struck

Tower it signalizes troubles from enemies. Under the sun on the card are two children, usually considered twins, who symbolize the "principle of ambivalence in the concept of duality which is the recurrent theme in the Major Arcana of the Tarot."[69] Duality or the "double" was one of Nerval's obsessions, as it was of Musset and Baudelaire. But the sun here is black (as in "Le Point noir"), and Nerval suggests that its life-giving, inspiration-giving aspects (his lute bears it) are no longer present. Thus, no matter what interpretation one gives to the first quatrain, it is evident that the sense of loss, displacement, and abandonment are clearly expressed.

The second quatrain reads, "In the night of the tomb, you who consoled me, give me back Posilipo and the Italian sea, the *flower* that so pleased my desolate heart, and the trellis where the vine is joined to the rose." Nerval is addressing a young English girl (Octavie) who he suggests saved him from suicide in 1834 in Italy. Posilipo, a mountain near Naples, supposedly contains Vergil's tomb, and, because of its two tunnels is reputedly the way Vergil led Dante into the underworld. The flower (although "ancolie," a symbol of sadness and madness, is written next to it in the margin of the Eluard manuscript) is obviously an oniric one representing something of significance that the poet remembers. However, he only suggests that it helped console him in a time of trouble. A slight note of hope sounds in this quatrain, for once before he had been brought out of his mental depression, and there is a possibility that this might happen again.

The personal element is continued in the tercets. Nerval relates, as in the second quatrain, events from his past as if he were searching for a way out of his present depression:

Am I Love or Phoebus? . . . Lusignan or Biron? My brow is still red from the kiss of the queen. I have dreamed in the grotto where the siren swims . . . And twice as conqueror I have crossed the Acheron, modulating in turn on Orpheus' lyre the sighs of the saint and the cries of the fairy.

In the first line the poet seeks his identity and wonders if he is Love or Phoebus, god of poetry and the sun, Lusignan, member of a feudal family founded by the fairy Mélusine, who appeared on the ramparts of the family castle to cry out impending misfortune, or Biron, subject of a Valois poem. The subject of creative power is renewed in this line. Is he lover or poet, noble or subject of poetry? Whatever he is, his brow is still burning from the kiss of the queen. Nerval is remembering a youthful experience, related in *Sylvie*, when Adrienne whom he loved, and who later became a nun, kissed him. This memory suggests that his poetic inspiration is still derived from past love. He has been inspired as well by the song of the sirens, and twice has crossed one of the rivers of hell (his two previous attacks of madness) singing, as conqueror, both mystical songs and magic ones: those of the saint—Adrienne, and those of the fairy—Mélusine, sirens.

But after the stated present desperation of the first quatrain, the events of the rest of the poem took place in the past. Nerval wonders about his creative powers—gone for lack of inspiration and love, and whether another descent into Hell will claim him permanently. There remains the question whether it is possible for him to create again, to once more find his inspiration. "El Desdichado," even without consulting the numerous footnotes in the critical editions, *means* on first reading. The suggestive richness of the allusions, the use of novel rhythmic and melodic devices (accents, punctuation), the poignant portrayal of a desperate state of mind make this poem one of the most delicate yet powerful in all of French literature.

"Myrtho" is another hermetic sonnet of great suggestive power. One version of it has the title "A J-y Colonna" (Italian for Jenny Colon), which reveals the identity of Myrtho and shows how she has become enshrined in Nerval's personal Pantheon. Myrtho suggests myrtle, the flower sacred to Venus and therefore representative of love. The poet thinks of her as a divine enchanter, of the thousand fires shining on Posilipo, of Myrtho's face inundated with the brightness of the East, of the black grapes in her golden hair. Nerval relates that he has tasted rapture in her cup (the union of Venus and Bacchus) and in her smiling eyes while he was praying to Bacchus for, he says, "the Muse has made me one of Greece's sons."[70] The two quatrains relate a sense of ecstasy, a freedom given by love

and wine, a reveling in an ancient rite. This state of mind
had been present in the past, but memory has fixed it in the
present. In Greek esoterica, Bacchus-Dionysus was identified
with Osiris as ruler of the nether world, the realm of fire.[71] The
grapes suggest the Bacchantes, and their delirium is communicated to the poet. But although Nerval sees time as one, he is
aware of time breaks, and in the tercets changes the tone and
time. "I know why down there the volcano reopened. . . . Because
yesterday you touched it with your agile foot, and the horizon
was suddenly covered with ashes."[72] Like Nerval, Myrtho is a
child of fire and can cause it because of her divine powers.
This is an important link between her and the poet. But this
incident happened in the past and hence there is a slight
note of melancholy tempered only by the action reliving in
the poet's memory.

The second tercet is more difficult to interpret than the rest
of the poem, "Since a Norman Duke broke your clay idols,
under Vergil's laurel boughs the pale hydrangea is still united
with the green myrtle."[73] Nerval implies that a Norman Duke
tried to erase the traces of paganism in southern Italy, but still
in the shadow of Vergil, that is to say of poetry and the environs
of Naples itself, the pagan and Christian remain entwined as
do Christian love (the hydrangea is a symbol of faithful and
Christian love) and physical love (the myrtle).

"Myrtho" is a paean to the power of the myth of love and
the myth created by love. Its beauty is found in the color and
nobility of its language, the discreet presence of the poet,
and the evocative mingling of times, symbols, mythological
references and personal memories of the time he spent in
Naples with Octavie who has now become identified with Jenny
Colon in his mind.

"Horus," "Antéros," and "Artémis" are more mystical and
hermetic than the two previously discussed sonnets. These
poems are unlike anything that had previously been written
in French with the possible exception of several metaphysical
poems written in the early seventeenth century. Syncretism
dominates in these sonnets, and a knowledge of mythology and
religion comparable to Nerval's is necessary for an understanding of them. Horus was the son of Isis and Osiris, but the sonnet

has little relation to the Egyptian religion as such although Nerval may have learned or known while he was in Egypt many aspects of this religion of which we know little. In "Horus" there is a confusion between Kneph (Khnoum), a local god of Elephantine of great repute as a creator and who was supposed to have used the potter's wheel for this purpose, and Seth who murdered his brother Osiris, the father of Horus. Isis and Horus took their revenge on Seth, and Osiris became a fertility god (like Atys, Adonis, Dionysus) who was reborn every spring. Nerval's Kneph is a dying god, married to, and hated by, Isis who is identified in the poem as the Mother.

> The god Kneph, trembling, made the universe shudder.
> Isis, the mother, then arose from her couch
> Made a gesture of hatred at her ferocious spouse,
> And the ardor of old shone in her green eyes.
>
> "Do you see him?" she said, "This old pervert is dying.
> All the winters of the world have passed through his mouth.
> Tie up his crooked foot; put out his squinting eye.
> He's the god of volcanoes and king of winter!
>
> The eagle has already passed; the new spirit calls me.
> I have donned for him the robe of Cybele . . .
> He is the well-beloved child of Hermes and Osiris!"
>
> The goddess had fled on her gilded shell.
> The sea sent us back her adored image,
> And the heavens shone under Iris' scarf.[74]

In "Horus," as in *Voyage en Orient* and others of his works, Nerval sees Isis as the prefiguration of all the goddess mothers. Her function is to protect and inspire love. Kneph is identified in "Horus" with Ammon Ra, the creator of the universe. He is dying, and a new order is about to come into being through the birth of Horus, god of the sun and spring. The cyclical nature of time and being, an aspect of Nerval's Pythagorean concepts, plays an important role in this syncretic poem in which the gods of Egypt and Greece are intermingled and are part of a single unity. Even the rainbow (Iris's scarf) is reminiscent of the Bible and the covenant between God and Noah.

The contrasts in the sonnet between winter and spring, between death and life, between the old and new are clearly presented even though some of the imagery is obscure. "The eagle has already passed" is somewhat confusing, but in another version of the poem, "A Louise d'Or., Reine," the ninth line reads, "The eagle has already passed: Napoleon calls me."[75] Nerval, who, especially in his states of madness, identified with Napoleon, thought of the former Emperor as a demigod which might explain the symbol of the eagle and also suggest that Napoleon or Napoleon/Nerval was the new Horus. But the sonnet remains basically a poem of revolt, of change to a new world order under the influence of the goddess-mother Isis.

"Horus" is the least successful of the *Chimères*. There is padding in some of the lines (e.g., the *alors* in line 2), and the "ouche" sounds in the quatrains (*couche, farouche, bouche, louche*), while expressing the scorn of the goddess, remain basically ugly. "Horus" also has a psychological weakness. The person to whom Isis is speaking would certainly know that Kneph is the god of volcanoes and king of the winter, especially if Kneph is the god-creator. This line (8) is another example of padding, and it makes little psychological sense. Even in the most difficult poems of Nerval there is always an internal logic, but this is apparently lacking in "Horus." It is possible that this sonnet was written before the other *Chimères*, before Nerval had achieved his mastery of style and content.

"Antéros," in contrast, is one of the finest sonnets in the collection. It is a poem of rage and defiance and as such is more dramatic than lyric. Antéros, the brother of Eros and son of Aphrodite and Ares, was the god of offended love who punished those who did not respond to it. But Antéros might also mean contrary to love. In any case, the title suggests the theme of the poem which is not completely clarified until the final tercet.

> You ask why I have so much rage in my heart
> And an unbowed head on a pliable neck;
> It's because I am of the race of Antaeus;
> I hurl back the darts against the conquering god.

Yes, I am one of those whom the Avenger inspires;
He has marked my brow with his angry lip.
Beneath the pallor of Abel, alas, covered in blood,
I sometimes have the implacable redness of Cain.

Jehovah! the last one, conquered by your genius,
Who, from the depths of hell, cried out, "O tyranny!"
Is my ancester Bélus or my father Dagon . . .

They plunged me three times in the waters of the Cocytus,
And all alone protecting my mother Amalek
I sow again at her feet the teeth of the old dragon.[76]

Antéros is one of those exiled from God, as Nerval felt himself
to be. He is one of the race of Cain, of Antaeus the giant, who,
each time he felt overcome by Hercules, recovered his strength
by touching the ground, of Bélus and Dagon, Philistine fertility
gods of the Old Testament. Like the other characters mentioned in the poem, Antéros is of the earth and an opponent
of the monotheistic Judeo-Christian god. Like them, he too
bears the mark of Cain.

The syncretism in "Antéros" is seen in the mixing of mythologies so that Jehovah's opponents are not only Hebrew (Cain),
but Greek (Antaeus, Antéros) and non-Hebrew Semites (Bélus,
Dagon), all of whom were overthrown by the reigning god.
As in "El Desdichado" and the Adoniram section of *Voyage
en Orient,* the poet identifies with the disinherited, with the
proud victims of an irrational deity. They are men defeated,
but they find their *raison d'être* in their constant hostility to,
and hatred of, the conquering god. These rebels are symbolized
by earth and fire, the two elements most important in Nerval's
thought.[77]

The sonnet moves forcefully from beginning to end as the
cold rage of the speaker is tempered only by his defense and
self-justification. The poem begins with a question and then
provides the answers. The movement from rage to scorn and
defiance is capped by the last line. In it the vanquished one is
planting the seeds of a new race which will overthrow the
existing order. The connections between the Cainite revolt and
the god of offended love are initially somewhat difficult to

see, but Nerval is a victim of love and identifies with Antéros rather than Eros. He is revolting against the god that approves not of pagan love, but rather only of Christian love, a theme that is repeated in *Aurélia*.

"Artémis" is the most hermetic of the *Chimères*, and yet it is not only one of the finest poems of Nerval but, in many ways, like *Aurélia*—although in a more disciplined form—it is the summation of his life, dreams, thoughts, and love. The first quatrain indicates the problems in interpreting the sonnet:

> The Thirteenth returns . . . It (she) is still the first;
> And it (she) is always the only one,—or it's the only moment:
> For are you Queen, o You! the first or last?
> Are you King, you the only or the last lover? . . .[78]

An immediate difficulty, because it is ambiguous in French, is the pronoun *ce* which can be translated in the first and second lines by either "it" or "she," depending on the meaning of the "Thirteenth."

In one of the manuscripts Nerval speaks of this poem as the Ballet of the Hours, and it is quite possible to interpret the sonnet from the point of view of time. The thirteenth hour is also the first, and thus time is cyclical—once twelve is reached the cycle begins again—but it is always the same, a unity of eternal return. There is no real hint of progression, for Nerval indicates that "it is always the only one, or . . . the only moment." Again, as in so many of his writings, chronological time has been abolished, and what is left is a world of fixed forms, memories, and desires that have achieved the quality of myth. But to limit the interpretation of the first two lines to time alone is to limit the incredible suggestive power of the sonnet. Time is certainly suggested and meant, but it must be remembered that Artemis is the goddess of the moon which has thirteen manifestations during the course of the year. Thirteen is also the number of death, death which repeats itself in Nerval's mind until the individual deaths of certain beloved women (Baronne de Feuchères, Adrienne, Jenny Colon) become one as they become part of his ideal female figure. Time fixes death in the realm of myth, and the beloved women, by being transformed into myth, serve a function similar to that of Artemis, Isis, and the Virgin Mary—that of intercessor for man, and, as is shown in *Aurélia*, especially for Nerval himself.

The difficulty reappears in the third and fourth lines. The identity of the Queen and King is doubtful. Multiple possibilities present themselves for the identification of the Queen—Artemis, of course, the virgin goddess, goddess of chastity; Adrienne whom the young Nerval crowned queen in *Sylvie*; Jenny Colon for whom Nerval wanted to write an opera libretto based on the Queen of Sheba, a subject that haunted him throughout his adult life. But they have all coalesced into one. Nerval wonders if they are both the first and last and only Queen and if he, the King, is their only or last lover.

An important aspect of the first quatrain is the use of absolutes and superlatives, which give the impression of fixity and stability that is tempered only by the use of the questions in the third and fourth lines after the affirmations of the first two. The three dots at the end of line four, as in so much of Nerval's work, lead the reader to a pause: a state of reverie is induced by the break in order to prepare the reader for the second quatrain:

> Love the one who loved you from the cradle to the grave;
> She whom I alone loved still loves me tenderly:
> It's Death—or the Dead Woman . . . O delight! o torment!
> The rose that she holds is the *Hollyhock*.

The verb "love" is in the plural in French (*aimez*) as opposed to the familiar *tu* in the last two lines of the first quatrain. Nerval here seems to be exhorting others to love their mother (or perhaps a goddess-intercessor with whom the mother is identified). The Mother, whether dead or alive, still loves her child in this world or in the one beyond. His own mother, whom he alone loved,[79] still loves him no matter what he has done, no matter what state of anxiety he is in, as evidenced by the last two lines of the first quatrain. But she is Death or the Dead Woman—Mother, Adrienne, Sophie, Jenny—all of whom have become one in the Nerval mythology. She is holding out the hollyhock which has either some arcane or personal significance to the poet because of his italicizing the word. In

the Eluard manuscript a note of Gérard next to this last line
reads "Philomène," and the name Rosalie appears next to the
first line of the first tercet:

Neopolitan saint with hands full of fire,
Rose with the violet heart, flower of Saint Gudule:
Have you found your cross in the desert of the heavens?

White roses, fall! you insult our Gods,
Fall, white phantoms, from your burning sky:
—The Saint of the abyss is more saintly to me!

Henri Lemaître in a note to this poem in the Garnier edition
remarks:

St. Philomène is not a Neapolitan saint, but her relics had been
transferred from Rome to Campanie at the beginning of the nineteenth
century. Gérard could also not have missed thinking of the analogy
Philomène (Greek) (the beloved) ... We borrowed from a note
from the catalogue of the Nerval Exposition (Bibliothèque Nationale,
1955, no. 297) the following remarks: "Philomène and Rosalie, Italian
saints, died, the first pierced by arrows for having refused the love
of Diocletian; the second burning with the same mystic love as Mary
Magdalen. Rosalie, a popular saint, was invoked in Naples against
the most diverse forms of cataclysms. In *Octavie* a figure of this
saint, crowned with violet roses, watches over the child of a Neopolitan gypsy who was something of a magician. In the mind of Nerval
the white rose of the preserved and completely celestial saint is
opposed to the violet rose of the *saint of the abyss.*" Finally, the
saint with the hollyhock is also an oniric incarnation of Aurélia:[80]

There is an opposition in the tercets, as there is in *Aurélia*,
between Christianity and the neopagan religions. Rosalie, like
so many of Nerval's heroines, is identified with fire (and the
setting is Naples with Vesuvius in the background). The poet
asks if she has found her cross in the desert of the skies. In
other words, he wonders if there is the promise of salvation in
the beyond. But in the final tercet this idea appears to be
negated. The white roses, symbol of forgiveness in Goethe's
Faust, insult "our gods"—the pagan deities by whom Nerval
was fascinated. The white roses are only white ghosts from a

flaming sky, one that either burns because it is in the process of destruction or because it destroys other religions. But for Nerval the saint of the abyss is holier, and he refuses the possibility of redemption through Christianity. He prefers Artemis, the saint of the abyss.

Despite its hermetic qualities, "Artémis" can be read with pleasure even without knowing all the allusions. Its evocative powers caused by the poet's anguish, questioning, and different states of mind (delight-torment), with their concomitant contradictions, are extraordinary. In these fourteen lines are all the major themes of *Aurélia*—love, mythology, death, chastity, religion, salvation; in fact, the whole of one man's human experience distilled into a sonnet. Although there are many questions and doubts in the poet's mind, as can be seen from the disjointed quality of the quatrains and tercets (especially seen in the punctuation), he ends the poem in a state of almost resigned rejection. He has chosen paganism and even the Christian St. Rosalie because in Naples Nerval associated the Isis cult with Christianity. The obsession with chastity is also evident in "Artémis." The women, whether Christian saints, pagan goddesses, or the mythologized women of Nerval's own life, are all symbols of purity which the poet loves in a non-carnal way. Carnality would rob women of their mythic qualities, and Nerval cannot live without his own myths.

Nerval was long considered a minor poet in France because of his slim poetic output, yet the ten or twelve acknowledged masterpieces surely put him in a class with Keats who is, and rightly so, thought of as a major poet. When one thinks that, apart from the titanic Hugo and the perfectionist Baudelaire, none of the French Romantic poets, despite their prolificacy, wrote more than a dozen major poems, many of which seem dated today, one wonders why Nerval for so long was denied the rank of a major poet. The explanation is perhaps simple, for Nerval's hermetic poetry was too inaccessible for his contemporaries and succeeding generations who saw in his work only the value of the charming but decidedly minor odelettes. The Surrealist poets of the twentieth century were the first to discover the beauty of the *Chimères* and saw in them, as well as in *Aurélia*, literary masterpieces that prefigured their own.

Nerval was, of course, a revolutionary poet. His early poems, charming as they are, are essentially standard Romantic statements of a poet's emotions. Yet they contain in seed the elements that later will be developed into a completely new way of viewing both the external and internal worlds. Obsessive emotions and hints of a subconscious world of archetypes and personal monsters that are sensed in the poems written before the *Chimères* come to full flower in the later poetry. In these poems of his maturity Nerval has created a new prosody, a new vocabulary, new imagery, and a new sensibility. Punctuation, which is used in the standard manner in the early poems, becomes as important in the later ones as the words it encloses. It defines not only the content of the poems, but the poet's state of mind as he creates them. It presents new rhythms, new accents, and presents to the reader new worlds of suggestion that have infinite reverberations. What is stated is sometimes difficult to understand; what is left unstated opens new areas of perception. Nerval's poetry, although the product of a consummate artist, is an open-ended form in which much is left to the imagination. As such, the reader becomes a creator who, through the poet's insights, creates himself and a universe of which he has previously been unaware.

CHAPTER 3

The Writer of Prose

I Voyage en Orient

O F the money Nerval made from his writings, most was
earned from his prose works. Primarily a journalist for
twenty years, he wrote much criticism and many occasional
pieces for Parisian publications. Yet, aside from his translations
and the work on the poets of the French sixteenth century, his
first complete book to be published was the *Voyage en Orient*
(1851), a work that would ordinarily be classified under the
heading of literature of travel. Many travel books were written
and published in the first half of the nineteenth century in France
as well as elsewhere in Europe. Lamartine and Chateaubriand
were but two of the French writers who wrote of their trips to
the Middle East, but their books, as well as those of other Romantic writers, are quite different from *Voyage en Orient* of
Nerval.

The rage for and fascination with the Orient, which to the
Romantic writers, artists, and musicians as well might mean
Spain, North Africa, and/or Greece and the Middle East, was
a characteristic of the mentality of the epoch. The struggle of
the Greeks for independence from the Turks, a cause popular-
ized most strongly by Byron who died at Missolonghi, was an
issue that aroused heated feelings in the liberal political climate
of the early decades of the nineteenth century. In the after-
math of the Napoleonic era, European writers tended to be more
politically liberal than many who wrote after 1840. But connected
with the humanitarianism and political liberalism was the lure
of the exotic, a fascination already found in writers of the eighteenth century. The mysterious world of the East, with its
traditions, customs, and arts that differed so greatly from those
of western Europe, was also the source of many of the world's

great religions of both the past and present. The religious aspect
exerted its influence on Chateaubriand whose works, especially
Le Génie du christianisme, were a major force in restoring to
favor the aesthetic values of Christianity. Other writers and
painters such as Delacroix, Decamps, Gautier, and Hugo were
more interested in the picturesque, the colorful details of an
alien but fascinating culture. None of them, however, despite
their lasting successes in literature and the fine arts, sought in
the Middle East what Nerval was seeking—specifically himself.
Even momentarily they did not become part of the cultures they
portrayed. They presented these cultures from the point of view
of the foreigner, of the observer who notes the piquant and often
obvious details of exotic civilizations. Nerval, too, was interested
in the detail, in the differences between cultures, but his work
demonstrates that he could, either through imagination or hallucination, identify with the ideas that created the cultures he
was describing, that he could become, temporarily at least,
a part of them and in them could find a spiritual home.

It is for this reason that Nerval's *Voyage en Orient* is one of
the more remarkable books of the Romantic period, for like so
many of his other works, this is a book of quest. Nerval the
poet, the mystic, and the man seeking in the East not only himself, but something that lies beneath all human consciousness,
something basic to humanity but which has been overlaid by
centuries of cultural alienation, looks for the sources of ethical
and mystical ideas and uses them either as proof of, or consolation for, his own dreams and beliefs. In some ways he is, thus,
a precursor of the comparative religionists of our own day.

Except for the first part of the work entitled "Vers l'Orient,"
the book is not in the form of a diary or journal, although certain
sections do bear a resemblance to these literary forms. *Voyage
en Orient* is essentially a portrayal of the writer's imagination
coming into contact with a picturesque and often mystic reality,
and the juxtaposition and often the combination of the two
give the work its unique and intriguing tone. Nerval is no
respecter of chronological time here any more than he is in his
other literary works; his time is that of memory, the dream, and
the imagination. Nor is he a respecter of place or actual events.
Many of the sites he describes—Cythera, for example—he never

visited, yet they are as real to him as if he had sojourned in them, for his readings and viewings of works of art became part of his reality, an imagined reality, but a reality all the same. What Nerval has read he has made his own, and there is little question of plagiarism for he often admits his debts to other writers or so skillfully incorporates into his work stories or events about which he has read that they take on completely new meaning and color.

Like Nerval's other works, *Voyage en Orient* can be read on many levels, but it is basically as a story of quest that it must be considered. Written over a period of at least seven years, the book deals essentially with the author's trip through Switzerland to Vienna, the Greek islands, Egypt, Syria, Lebanon, and Turkey. In reality the trip to Vienna took place in 1839, four years before the trip to the Middle East. During the seven years following the latter trip, Nerval wrote *Voyage en Orient,* much of which was published piecemeal in various journals. Thus, in the process of creation, the author's memory played an important role, and memory for Nerval tends to become a newly experienced reality. The events of the past, whether experienced or read about, serve mainly as a springboard for new perceptions.

Voyage en Orient is an artistic fusion of a travel journal, a work of some sociological pretensions, a study of religions, a recounting of stories and anecdotes in the manner of the *Thousand and One Nights*, and a work of personal quest. The fact that Nerval was able to combine all these elements into a cohesive and always intriguing narrative is a sign of his literary mastery. The structure of the book, although seemingly loose when first read, is quite well planned. This may account for the unimportance or negligence of chronological time sequences. It is divided into four parts: "Vers l'Orient," "Les Femmes du Caire," "Druses et Maronites," and "Les Nuits du Ramazan." At the beginning of the first part, Nerval describes his trip to Vienna and is mainly concerned with local color. Unlike the other Romantic writers, however, Nerval describes landscapes as if they were theatre settings: Nature is the Nature of art rather than of reality. Writing of the public promenade at Lausanne, he says:

From there the view is admirable. The lake extends to the right as far as the eye can see, sparkling in the light of the sun, while to the left it seems to be a river which becomes lost among the high mountains, dimmed by their great shadows. The snowy summits crown this operatic view, and at our feet, beneath the terrace, the yellowing vines unfold like a carpet to the edge of the lake. As an artist would say, there is the *stereotype* of Swiss nature; we find it all everywhere from ornamentation to water colors. The only thing lacking is the natives in costume.[1]

In landscapes Nerval prefers dreams or fantasy to reality:

I admit I looked for that bluish cathedral, those squares with sculptured houses, those bizarre and crooked streets, and that whole picturesque Middle Ages which our set designers at the Opéra had created so poetically. Well, all that was only dream and invention. Instead of Constance imagine Pontoise, and there we are closer to reality . . .
It is also a painful impression, as one goes further on, to lose, from city to city and country to country, that whole beautiful universe that one has created when he was young by means of readings, paintings, and dreams. The world that is thus created in the minds of children is so rich and so beautiful that one does not know if it is the result of learned ideas or if it is a remembrance of a former existence and the magic geography of an unknown planet.[2]

It is therefore not surprising to find in all of Nerval's prose writings, even those that pretend to be realistic, descriptions that are imprecise, dreamlike, exotic, and theatrical, and this fact accounts for much of the charm and magic of pieces such as *Voyage en Orient, Sylvie,* and *Aurélia.*

Much of the rest of "Vers l'Orient" gives an account of Nerval's amorous experiences in Vienna, a tale continued in the later *La Pandora.* In the first part of *Voyage en Orient,* then, Nerval is concerned mainly with himself and his reactions to his surroundings, and this section is essentially one of romanticized confessions. The picturesque dominates the second part, "Les Femmes du Caire," as the author relates his adventures in Cairo and presents material that is basically of the travel book variety. Much of it has its sources in the works of other authors.[3] In the third part, "Druses et Maronites," Nerval presents important and striking aspects of certain Eastern religions. The first climax of the book (the quest is almost theatrical in form) is reached in this section, for the author finds a sosie in Caliph Hakem as he investigates the religion and customs of the Druses. The major climax and the most interesting part of the book are found in the fourth section, "Les Nuits du Ramazan." Here Nerval relates the story, an understanding of which is essential for the study of his later works, of Solomon, Adoniram, and the Queen of Sheba. The movement from the first section to the last is from a romanticized reality to myth as an expression of a reality higher than that of Nerval's own earthly life and one to which he aspires. His identification in the last two sections with Caliph Hakem (who was or thought himself to be God) and Adoniram (the Cainite builder of Solomon's temple) brings him almost to the end of his spiritual quest, for even though these two men failed in the worldly sense (both were murdered), they had become figures of myth and had had knowledge and experience of love and religion unknown to most men. Nerval, who, like these two heroes, had experienced a great though unconsummated love and had an acute awareness of religions, relives their experiences as he describes them through the medium of storytellers.

In the letter to Alexandre Dumas that serves as a preface to *Les Filles du feu,* Nerval writes:

There are, you know, certain storytellers who cannot invent without identifying with the characters of their imagination. You know with what conviction our old friend Nodier told how he had the misfortune of being guillotined at the time of the Revolution. One became so persuaded by it that one wondered how he happened to glue his head back on. . . . Well, do you know that the development of a narrative can produce a similar effect, that one reaches the point, so to say, of incarnating oneself so well in the hero of one's imagination that his life becomes yours, and you burn with the factitious flames of his ambitions and loves.[4]

Nerval himself not only identifies with the characters of Hakem and Adoniram, but seems to become them because he gives them many of his own attributes, desires, dreams, and fantasies.

Nerval has created himself in their portraits, and in them finds
the object of his quest.

Hakem, the Caliph of Cairo, wanders in disguise through the
city every night. On one of his sorties he meets Yousouf who
offers him some hashish. The latter extols the virtues of the drug,
which Hakem says makes man like a god:

"Yes," replied Yousouf enthusiastically. "Water drinkers know only
the vulgar and material appearance of things. Intoxication, while
troubling the eyes of the body, clears those of the soul. The mind,
freed from the body, its weighty jailer, flees like a prisoner whose
guard, having left the key to the cell in the lock, has gone to sleep.
It wanders joyous and free in space and light, chatting familiarly
with the genii it meets who dazzle it with sudden and charming
revelations."[5]

Each man then relates the story of his love. Yousouf has a recurrent dream of a mysterious and beautiful woman who resembles
a goddess. One night, however, when not completely under the
influence of the drug, he saw her in reality:

"I had not dreamed," Yousouf continued ... "Haschish had only
caused a memory buried in the deepest part of my mind to come to
the surface, for this divine face was known to me. For example,
where had I already seen it? In what world had we met? What former
existence had brought us into contact?"[6]

The relationship between dreams and life, the coexistence of
different time spans, and predestined love were concerns of
Nerval throughout his career, and the all-pervasive religious tone
he brings to his treatment of these subjects is what distinguishes
his works from those of his contemporaries.

Hakem understands the experiences of his companion and,
in his turn, tells of the great love of his life—his sister.[7] Hakem
sounds much like Nerval speaking of Aurélia when he relates
that his love is completely pure and that it transcends time:

"My love has none of the earthly impurities. It is not voluptuousness
which attracts me to my sister even though she equals in beauty the
phantom of my visions. It is an indefinable attraction, an affection

deep as the sea, vast as the heavens, one that a god could experience. The idea that my sister could be united to a man inspires disgust and horror in me as if it were a sacrilege. In her there is something celestial at which I guess through the veils of the flesh. In spite of her earthly name she is the wife of my divine soul, the virgin destined for me from the beginning of creation. Sometimes I believe I have recaptured appearances of our secret filiation across the ages and the shadows. Scenes which happened before the appearance of men on the earth come back to me in memory, and I see myself under the golden boughs of Eden seated next to her and served by obedient spirits. By uniting myself to another woman I would fear prostituting and dissipating the soul of the world which pulsates within me."[8]

Others in the group in which Hakem finds himself begin to sacrifice a white cock to Hermes, and he calls them blasphemers and idolators. Asked whom he worships, he replies, "I adore no one since I myself am God, the only one, the true one, the sole one, of whom the others are only shadows."[9] He is attacked physically for his own blasphemy, but is saved by Yousouf who rows him back to his island.

Convinced that he is God not only when he is under the influence of hashish, he is addressed as such by a mysterious blind man who reappears at various times and seems to be the voice of his own conscience. When he again takes the drug, he returns to his palace in a strange and frenzied state, goes to his sister, and announces that he will marry her in three days. She is shocked and tells the Grand Vizier Argévan, who claims that Hakem has gone insane. Argévan, fearful of the loss of his own power, surprises Hakem while he is taking hashish and claims that he is not the Caliph, but an imposter. Imprisoned in a madhouse, Hakem, not unlike Nerval, experiences moments of lucidity as well as moments of hallucination:

If mortals cannot conceive by themselves what happens in the soul of a man who suddenly feels himself to be a prophet or of a mortal who feels himself to be God, Fable and history have at least permitted them to suppose what doubts, what anguish must be produced in these divine natures in the vague epoch when their intelligence frees itself from the transitory bonds of incarnation. At moments Hakem had doubts about himself like the Son of Man on the Mount of Olives, and what especially astonished him was the idea that his divinity had been first revealed to him in the ecstacies of hashish. "There exists, therefore," he thought, "something greater than He who is all. Could it be that an herb of the fields could create such marvels? It is true that a simple worm proved that he was stronger than Solomon when it pierced through and broke the middle of the staff on which this prince of the genii had leaned. But what is Solomon next to me if I am really Albar (the Eternal)?"[10]

Freeing himself from the madhouse, Hakem resumes his rule. One day he finds that his palace is in a state of festivity, and he is astounded when he sees his sister entertaining his double:

This vision seemed to him to be a celestial warning, and his trouble increased when he recognized, or believed he did, his own features in those of the man seated next to his sister. He believed it was his *ferouer* or his double, and for the Easterners seeing one's own ghost is a sign of ill omen.[11]

This scene of the marriage of the double brings up a tantalizing problem. In *Aurélia* Nerval, in one of his hallucinations, also witnesses the preparations for the marriage of his double to Aurélia. Was Nerval remembering seven years later the story he had told in *Voyage en Orient*, or had he himself had this hallucination and transferred it to Hakem? One of the problems with certain of the author's works is that it is often difficult to discover where reality begins and where it turns into fiction, dream, or hallucination. The boundaries are vague and often indefinable for Nerval was a creature of obsessions that recur with startling regularity throughout his works.

The story ends abruptly when, after discovering that Yousouf is his double, Hakem is killed by three men, one of whom is Yousouf who, upon recognizing Hakem, tries to defend him and, in so doing, is killed himself. The self has been reintegrated in death, and the god has escaped from his earthly prison. This story of the Caliph-God is also the story of Nerval, for Hakem is his spiritual double, victim of madness and hallucinations, prey to an impossible love, and, temporarily at least, believer in his own godhead. Both this section of the *Voyage en Orient* and the later part dealing with Adoniram should be read in conjunction with *Aurélia*, for they illuminate and clarify certain aspects of each other. In *Aurélia* Nerval takes on—perhaps they were his to begin with—certain traits of both Hakem and Adoniram, but these similarities are clouded by Nerval's own account of his madness.

Nerval's portrayal of the adventures and thoughts of Hakem not only has much force and intensity, but also the personal poignancy of a man seeking himself and never being completely assured of his identity. The style becomes more intense and concentrated, more emotional even, as the story continues, and it, as well as the subject, demonstrates that the author has undergone many of the same trials as the character he has created in his own likeness. An excellent and compelling psychological portrait, the story of Hakem tells the reader much about the states of mind of a man who sees beyond our reality, or what we accept as such, and, as well, a good deal about the process of artistic creation in the mind of Nerval.

The subject of the Queen of Sheba had intrigued Nerval at least since the early 1830's, and he supposedly wrote a libretto for Meyerbeer about this Eastern Queen. The role was to have ben sung by Jenny Colon, but somehow the opera was not written, and Nerval's libretto has not been discovered. The account of the subject that Nerval presents in *Voyage en Orient* seems, because of the dominance of theatrical dialogue in certain sections, to have been derived from the missing libretto. Ironically, an opera based on Nerval's prose story in "Les Nuits du Ramazan" entitled *Histoire de la Reine du Matin et de Soliman, Prince des Génies* (*Story of the Queen of the Morning and of Solomon, Prince of the Genii*) was produced in 1862 with a libretto by Barbier and Carré and music by Gounod.[12] Nerval's prose tale of over one hundred pages reads like a novella, of which it has the basic form, and it is without doubt one of the most Romantic of the author's works.

The major character, Adoniram, builder of Solomon's temple, is brother to the Byronic heroes. He is a creative genius. He has great beauty and his most dominant trait, his flashing eyes, has the ability to transfix people. He is somber, mysterious, of unknown origin, rebellious, and lonely. He says several times that, apart from his work, he has fled the society of men. Adoniram is the incarnation of one type of Romantic hero and

Nerval's mystic ideal for he is aware of, and able to create, a reality beyond that of the earth, the reality of the artist and the mystic. Balkis, the Queen of Sheba, sees him as the god of fire, and Nerval, who also felt himself to be a child of fire, makes of him a Cainite, a descendent of Cain and therefore a rebel against Adonai, the Hebrew God worshipped by Solomon. Adoniram's ancestor Tubal Cain takes him on a journey to the center of the earth to the palace of Enoch where the Cainites dwell. He tells the artist:

You have reached the domain of your fathers. Here the line of Cain rules alone. Under these granite fortresses, in the middle of these inaccessible caverns, we have been able finally to find freedom. Here the jealous tyranny of Adonai dies, here it is that one can, without dying, subsist on the fruits of the Tree of Knowledge.[13]

Solomon is a child of the earth, a worshipper of Adonai. He is vain, arrogant, deceitful, and determined to have Balkis as wife. Throughout the story, this king who accepts the *status quo* is parodied by Nerval in the person of Balkis who demonstrates that Solomon's proverbial wisdom is essentially empty. The underlying conflict between him and Adoniram is basically that of the yes-sayer versus the rebel, of the traditionalist versus the creator. Solomon is the classicist fighting romantic art which, in the person of Adoniram, is based on the imagination and the dream. Solomon says:

It is said that there, in the accursed countries, one sees surge up the debris of the impious city submerged by the waters of the Flood, the vestiges of the criminal Enochia . . . constructed by the gigantic descendents of Tubal. It is the city of the children of Cain. Anathema on that art of impiety and shadows! Our new temple reflects the brightness of the sun; its lines are simple and pure, and the order and unity of the plan translate the straightforwardness of our faith . . .[14]

Adoniram, the romantic and the ideal of Nerval, has quite different ideas about art. His assistant Benoni tells the sculptor that he is always dreaming of the impossible. Adoniram replies:

We were born too late; the world is old, and old age is infirm . . . Decadence and downfall! You copy nature coldly; you keep busy like the housewife who is weaving a veil of flax. Your vacant mind becomes in turn the slave of a cow, a lion, a horse, a tiger, and the object of your work is vying, through imitation, with a heifer, a lioness, a tigress, a mare; . . . these animals do what you execute, and even more, for they pass on life with form. Child, art is not there. Art consists of creating. When you sketch one of those ornaments which curves throughout the friezes do you limit yourself to copying the flowers and foliage that trail along the ground? No. You invent. You let your stylet follow the whim of your imagination and blend together the most bizarre fantasies. Well, beside portraying existing man and animals, why don't you also seek unknown forms, unnamed beings, incarnations before which man has drawn back, dreadful couplings, figures suited for inspiring respect, gaiety, amazement, and fear? Remember those ancient Egyptians and the bold and naive artists of Assyria. Didn't they tear from flanks of granite those sphinxes, those cynocephali, those divinities of basalt whose sight revolted the Jehovah of old David? On reseeing these formidable symbols from age to age people will repeat that bold geniuses formerly existed. Were those people dreaming of form? They scoffed at it, and, strong in their inventions, they could cry out to Him who created all: "You don't understand these granite beings, and you would not dare to make them come to life." But the multiple God of nature has bent you under the yoke. Matter limits you. Your degenerate genius immerses itself in the vulgarities of form. Art is lost.[15]

There is more to the world than what is immediately visible, and the artist must rely on instinct, emotion, visions, and the dream for his creations. Hud-Hud, the hoopoe bird belonging to Balkis, and Balkis herself, another child of fire, are aware of a supernatural world that may become the subject of art, a world that is alien to Solomon.

Balkis has come to Jerusalem to hear Solomon's wisdom and admire the marvels of his temple, but she is immediately attracted to Adoniram, and they eventually experience a physical but also mystic love that has been predetermined from the beginning of time. After Adoniram's murder, she returns to Sheba carrying his child who will become a great king of the line of the Cainites. Although she is better characterized in both speech and action than most of Nerval's other female creations who are basically wraiths, she is still the goddess to Nerval, and therefore there is more psychological penetration into the character of Adoniram who dominates the piece. In Adoniram Nerval is describing himself, perhaps as he would like to be, perhaps as he thinks he is, and, despite the fictional devices which, of necessity, separate him from his hero, he finds his ideal in Adoniram.

Many of Nerval's obsessions are in evidence in this story. There is a strong element of syncretism in the author's depiction of religions. Judaism, the Egyptian religion, the mystic rites of the Masons, and the Cainite religion are all found in this story. Solomon, the obedient servant of Adonai, sees in Balkis "the ideal and mystic figure of the goddess Isis." Balkis thus is the eternal woman, the goddess who goes by many names and takes many forms in Nerval's works. The Masonic Tau is used by Adoniram to assemble the workers on the temple, and it is as well the sign of the Cainites. Perhaps the most important aspect of Nerval's depiction of Judaism is the constant attacks on organized religions that are intolerant of others. The portrayal of Judaism as an intolerant religion foreshadows Nerval's later attacks on Christianity which, to him, had destroyed all the beauties of the pagan world.

The section of the story that describes Adoniram's journey to the center of the earth again presents the Nervalian preoccupation with the conflict between reality and the dream or the hallucination. Nerval, describing the beginning of the trip, writes, "The more they advanced in the profound region of silence and night, the more Adoniram doubted himself and the reality of his impressions."[16] On his return to earth, Adoniram says:

"A dream! . . . was it then a dream? . . . What is only too true is the loss of my hopes, the ruin of my projects, and the dishonor that awaits me at daybreak . . ."

But the vision is recalled with such clarity that he is suspicious of the very doubt by which he is seized.[17]

The journey to the land of the Cainites may well have been an hallucination, but its reality is so vivid, both to Adoniram and in Nerval's description, that the whole concept of reality is put into question.

Another major theme in Nerval's works is that of the eternal woman and the love that can exist between her and a man.

Nerval here portrays the union of the ideal male and female with brilliance. The Queen of Sheba prefigures the goddess-woman of Nerval's later works, but Adoniram is not the predecessor of the Nerval of *Sylvie, Octavie* or *Aurélia*. He is too strong, too untainted by guilt to be the sad, guilt-ridden personage of these other stories. As such he represents an ideal to which Nerval aspires rather than Nerval himself. It is as if for once in his works Nerval is seriously looking at, and creating, what he would like to be rather than what he is.

II *Excursions and Memories*

Nerval, himself, is the main character in *Les Nuits d'octobre*, which appeared in *L'Illustration* from October 9 to November 13, 1852. The work, he relates, is to be an attempt at realism à la Dickens, and there are connections in content and style between it and *Les Nuits de Paris* of Restif de la Bretonne. Nerval had read several pages of translation from Dickens in the *Revue brittanique*. He writes:

How fortunate the English are to be able to write and read chapters of observation stripped of all the alloys of romanesque invention! In Paris we would be asked to have anecdotes and sentimental stories strewn throughout the work—ending either with a death or a marriage. The realistic intelligence of our neighbors is satisfied with the absolute truth.[18]

He continues by asking whether the novel will ever render the effects of the bizarre combinations of life. Although Nerval intends to write *Les Nuits d'octobre* in the style he mentions in the above quotation, he moves from realism to fantasy throughout the work and often achieves his own peculiar blend of the two styles. An example of his realism is the chapter entitled "Mon Ami" which, borrowing a certain stylistic tone from Diderot, presents an excellent characterization of his friend Auguste de Châtillon. There is much picturesque detail in the description which deals with the bizarre psychological characteristics of the man rather than his physical appearance. Yet in the succeeding chapter, "La Nuit de Montmartre," a description of quarrymen is followed by the abrupt intrusion of Nerval's own fantasy:

Unfortunately the great quarries are closed today. There was one near the Château-Rouge which seemed to be a Druid temple with its high pillars supporting the square arches. One's eyes plunged into the depths from which one trembled to see appear Esus or Thot or Cérunnos, the formidable gods of our fathers.[19]

Les Nuits d'octobre is almost the rambling travel journal of a man who has missed his train and then wanders about Paris experiencing the adventures which he recounts in a light tone. He sees the city as circles of hell and mentions Dante quite often, but the inhabitants of this inferno do not have the memorable qualities or individuality of the characters of the Italian master or, for that matter, of Dickens. The work is not as powerful as Restif's either, in part because Nerval, though not prudish, is quite discreet, although colorful, is never piquant.

Yet the realistic details provide much pleasure as well as information about the low life of Paris at night. Nerval writes twice of the daguerreotype as an instrument of realism, one to which he would like the technique of his observations to be compared:

... on the fourth floor the daguerreotype, an instrument of patience which appeals to tired minds and which, destroying illusions, shows to each face the mirror of truth.[20]

If all these details were not exact, and if I were not seeking here to daguerreotype truth what novelistic resources these two types of misfortune and brutalization would furnish me![21]

Yet, despite the realism of parts of the work, *Les Nuits d'octobre* contains a dream that Nerval has experienced, one quite reminiscent of those found in *Aurélia*. In this section we move from observation and notation to the description of the personal world of dreams and their symbols:

Corridors—endless corridors! Stairs—stairs that one goes up, comes down, goes up again, steps of which the bottom one is always soaking in a black water that is agitated by wheels ... Going up, coming down or going through corridors—and all that for several eternities ... Could it be the punishment to which I would be condemned for my faults?[22]

Following the description of the dream in a chapter entitled "Réflexions," the tone changes again. In this chapter we find what might be considered a definite predecessor of the technique of stream-of-consciousness:

Let's recompose our memories.

I am of age and vaccinated. My physical qualities are of little import for the moment. My social position is superior to that of the circus performer of last night,—and, decidedly, his Venetian woman will not marry me.

A feeling of thirst is coming over me.

Returning to the *Mars* café at this hour would be wanting to walk on the remains of an extinguished firework.

Moreover nobody can yet be up there. Let's wander along the banks of the Marne and by those terrible water mills whose memory troubled my sleep.

Those mills with their slate roofs, so somber and noisy by moonlight, must be full of charm in the rays of the rising sun.[23]

In the next chapter, "La Femme mérinos," Nerval returns to objective realism although he begins the chapter by saying, "The profession of *realist* is too hard. The reading of an article of Dickens is moreover the source of these divagations! . . . A serious voice calls me back to myself."[24] He continues:

I've just drawn from beneath several Parisian and *Marnoise* newspapers a feuilleton from which an anethema exhales with reason on the bizarre imaginations which today constitute the *school of the true*.

The same movement existed after 1830, after 1794, after 1716 and after many other previous dates. People, tired of political or novelistic conventions, wanted the *true* at any price.

Now the true is the false, at least in art and poetry. What is falser than the *Iliad*, the *Aeneid*, *Jerusalem Delivered*, the *Henriade*, than tragedies, than novels?[25]

Therefore, in art and literature there is no such thing as the "true" because art is always an artifice and never real life as it is lived from moment to moment. The attempt to impose a form on reality, and all art has some sort of form, immediately raises that reality to the level of artifice, and compared with the "true" that is the basis of that artifice the ordered reality is false. Nerval ends his book with this statement:

There is the faithful story of three October nights which corrected for me the excesses of too absolute a realism. At least I have grounds for hoping so.[26]

Les Nuits d'octobre is a rambling, discursive work that has little unity. Its charm lies in the anecdotes related by Nerval and the lightness of tone in which they are told. The work is of interest, too, however, because the concept of realism and the many digressions about art itself tell us much about Nerval's point of view in fiction. Three fictional styles are attempted—realism, impressionism, and stream-of-consciousness—and all three are successful pastiches or predecessors of those styles. *Les Nuits d'octobre* is a minor work, but, like so many of Nerval's less important works, it has charm and tells a good deal about the author's process of thought and creation.

Petits Châteaux de Bohème (1853) is a polymorphous work that was originally called *La Bohème galante*. It is a series of writings in the form of poetry and anecdotal prose which evokes the nostalgia Nerval feels for the days when he had lived a bohemian life in the heyday of Romanticism in the artistic milieu of the Impasse du Doyenné. It is a typically Nervalian work in the sense that it contains, in flower or in seed, most of the major themes of his works and many of his lifelong obsessions. Dedicated to Arsène Houssaye, *Petits Châteaux de Bohème* is an answer to the editor's query about some of Nerval's poetry, and, in turn, it evokes an earlier period of his life.[27] Like many of his works in prose this book is in part autobiographical and in part the product of his creative rather than retentive memory.

The title indicates the tenor of the book. The adjective "small" or "little" indicates a modesty on the part of the poet with regard to his past achievements in both life and literature. The word "Châteaux" is important in the Nervalian vocabulary because the château (as in "Fantaisie") becomes almost a symbol of longing for the past, for youth, for the dream. In *Petits Châteaux de Bohème* there are three major châteaux: the château de Bohème, the castle in Spain, and the château of cards. All have become castles in air, but they are remembered even though they have physically disappeared.

Aside from the charm of the reminiscences and anecdotes and

the interest of the poetry (which has already been discussed),[28] the work contains important personal comments about Nerval's art. He writes to Houssaye in the dedication:

I send you the three ages of the poet; there is no longer in me anything but a stubborn prose writer. I wrote the first poems in the enthusiasm of youth, the second through love, the last through despair ... The Muse entered my heart like a goddess with golden words; she escaped from it like a pythoness screaming with pain. But her last sounds became more gentle as she disappeared. She turned back for one instant, and I saw again, as in a mirage, the adored traits of former days.[29]

He continues by saying that the life of the poet is the life of all and claims it is useless to define all its phases.

In the first château—Bohème—he remembers and describes the visual aspects of his friends working and playing, the balls they held, the suppers they gave, and their costume parties. These latter are described in almost eighteenth-century terms which are like graceful, languorous verbal equivalents of the paintings of Watteau. But the past gave way to the future, for Nerval remarks, "Our palace has been razed,"[30] and the paintings of which he and his friends were so proud have all but disappeared. In this section the sense of loss is a counterpoint to the happy memories that will be continued throughout the work.

One of the subjects that fascinated Nerval during his life was an important preoccupation in those youthful days. Inspired by his passion for the singer Jenny Colon, he was going to write a libretto for Meyerbeer on the subject of the Queen of Sheba:

The startling phantom of the daughter of the Hémiarites tormented my nights under the tall columns of the large sculpted bed bought in Touraine ... *She* appeared radiant to me, as on the day when Solomon admired her as she advanced towards him in the crimson splendors of morning. She came to propose to me the eternal enigma that the Wise Man could not resolve, and her eyes, which were animated by mischievousness rather than love, alone tempered the majesty of her Oriental face. How beautiful she was! Not more beautiful, however, than another queen of morning whose image tormented my days. This latter living woman brought to reality my ideal and divine dream. She had, like the immortal Balkis, the gift communicated by the miraculous hoopoe. The birds were quiet on hearing her songs, ... [31]

Jenny Colon was Nerval's Queen of Sheba, and in that guise as well as others she was to haunt him until his death. It is questionable whether the libretto was finished, but the story of the Queen of Sheba appears in the Adoniram section of *Voyage en Orient* and is one of the most fascinating and important parts of that work. In the "Second Château," Nerval recounts the story of the libretto he wrote for Meyerbeer, but, not being used, it was later transformed into the "Nuits du Ramazan." "Thus poetry turned into prose," Nerval writes,[32] and his theatrical château constructed with frame, beams, and practicables fell.

Regret is another subject Nerval discusses in the "Premier Château." Characteristic of his psychological problems with women, regret always appears when he is in contact with the beloved or someone who might be loved by him. He discusses an encounter at a party with a woman in tears whom he attempted to console and relates their adventures. Although he could undoubtedly have pursued the affair, he left the woman with friends and later regretted it. Again a sense of loss: "I had left the prey for the shadow—as always."[33]

In the last prose section of the "Premier Château," Nerval recounts how he wrote his early poetry. He says he wrote à la Ronsard, the Renaissance poet's *Odes* serving him as a model. He notes the musical qualities of these works, for they were songs as were the ancient odes. One, "Les Cydalises," came to him in the form of a song, and he wrote both the words and the melody. There follow in the text the poems he wrote at this period of his life.

The "Second Château," discussed above, is only three paragraphs long, and it was followed originally by the proverb *Corilla* which Nerval later published in *Les Filles du Feu*. The "Troisième Château," the house of cards, is the third of at least seven through which all poets must pass before they attain the famous château of brick and stone dreamed of by them in their youth. But, Nerval comments, few arrive there. It is the same château described in "Fantaisie," and in it is the muse, the poet's inspiration. Nerval, himself, while waiting to attain it, passed through the devil's château, an allusion to his mental breakdown of 1841. The prose section of the "Troisième Château" ends on a note similar to that of the beginning of the second part of *Aurélia*: his beloved is lost forever. The poetry which follows was conceived in fever and insomnia. It began in despair and ended in resignation. "Then a purified breath of first youth returns, and several poetic flowers open again in the form of the beloved odelette,— to the skipping rhythm of an opera orchestra."[34] There follow two groups of poems, one entitled "Mysticisme," which includes the "Vers dorés," "Daphné," and "Le Christ aux oliviers" which were later included in *Les Chimères,* the other entitled "Lyricisme," which contains verses he wrote for operas.

Petits Châteaux de Bohème achieves a unity only through the presence of Nerval himself in the work. It is a sort of sporadic *vie intime* of the poet who is attempting to explain the situations and events, both external and internal, that gave rise to his poetry. As in most of Nerval's lyrical prose works, there is found in *Petits Châteaux de Bohème* much charm, a sense of fantasy, a wistful atmosphere, and elegantly limpid prose.

III   *The Eternal Woman*

Les Filles du feu, published in 1854, is, at first glance, a work haphazardly thrown together: it is basically a collection of prose narratives, essays, a one-act play, and the poetry called *Les Chimères.* The various parts of this apparently hybrid work date from the late 1830's to the date of publication, a period of over fifteen years. Some of the individual works had been published before, a few several times in slightly different versions. *Sylvie,* the last written, had been published in 1853 in the *Revue des Deux Mondes*; *Octavie* in its first form had been published in 1842; *Corilla* had seen print several times and was included in the *Petits Châteaux de Bohème. Isis,* an adaptation of a German archaeological work on the Temple at Pompeii, had first appeared in *La Phalange* in 1845. To these were added *Angélique,* which is related to Nerval's study of the Abbé de Bucquoy, which appeared in *Les Illuminés.* Two other prose works were also in the collection: *Jemmy,* a translation of a German story, and *Emilie,* whose authenticity is dubious. A long essay entitled *Chansons et légendes du Valois* and *Les Chimères* completed the work.

What first seems to be a hodgepodge of loosely organized

material is actually a well-organized book with a unity of its own. If we except the spurious works *Jemmy* and *Emilie*, we find that the first three prose works, *Angélique, Sylvie*, and *Chansons et légendes du Valois*, form a group that deals with France, its history, its folklore, and especially with Nerval's beloved Valois. *Octavie, Isis*, and *Corilla* all have Naples and its environs for setting and are germane thematically as well as geographically. The pendant of *Les Chimères* completes the work, and each of the sonnets, discussed elsewhere,[35] continues the tones set by the preceding prose works.

But the unity of the work is to be found in the character of Nerval himself, for *Les Filles du feu* is really a spiritual autobiography of the writer, an autobiography soon after to be completed by *La Pandora* and *Aurélia*. The work is not only a sentimental journey through Nerval's amorous life from childhood to the epoch of his infatuation with Jenny Colon, but a journey through poetic time and place, the time of childhood, the time of memory, the time of contemplation, the time of dream. All these forms of time are placed in, or fundamentally related to, two places: his native Valois and Naples. What remain individual instances of reality in the prose portions of the book become, in *Les Chimères*, fused into a timeless world in which chronological time has little or no place. The Valois and the Neopolitan become one in the poet's mind, and he transfixes his experiences into his own personal myth. The world of childhood and its magic, the fascination of folklore and legends, religion with its mystic charm and awe, and love, which plays a role in each of these, are the main interests of Nerval and the basic subjects of this work.

Fire, as has been seen, played an important part in the imagination of Nerval, and the women who people this collection are daughters of fire. The fire may be that of love inspired either in them as in *Angélique*, or in the poet as in *Sylvie, Octavie*, or *Corilla*. The fire of Vesuvius, always in the background yet always present in the three works that have Naples as décor, recalls the fire of religions of the ancient world as well as Vergil and Dante.

Angélique consists of twelve letters written to the Director of the *National* and is a work that somewhat resembles certain pieces of Diderot and Sterne. The unity in this rambling work (the longest in *Les Filles du feu*) is Nerval's search for a book on the Abbé de Bucquoy which leads him to the many digressions that all have some bearing on the basic story. Jean Richer sees the work as having a musical structure,[36] as a concerto for piano and orchestra in three movements, and Nerval himself suggests a symphonic form in the tenth letter:

Just as it is good even in a pastoral symphony to have the principal motif, be it gracious, tender, or frightening, return from time to time in order to make it finally thunder forth at the finale with the graduated tempest of all the instruments,—I believe it useful to speak to you again of the Abbé de Bucquoy . . .[37]

The structure of the story is loose, however, and the interest of the reader often falters in the descriptions of Nerval's peregrinations in the country near Paris—Senlis, Châalis, Ermenonville—in his quest for knowledge about the Abbé. The first three letters constitute a sort of prelude which introduces the object of the search for the book on de Bucquoy's life; the next six deal, with many digressions, with the history of a member of the Abbé's family, Angélique de Longueville, and the last three with the results of the search and descriptions of the countryside and its manners.

While he was in Frankfort Nerval had come across a copy of a book on the life of the Abbé de Bucquoy, but, confident that he can find the book in Paris, does not buy it. He searches Parisian bookstores and libraries for the book because he wants to write about the Abbé. His searches seem to be in vain. Most leads on the work end up as futile excursions although he is alerted to a sale of a collection in which the work is to be found, and, at the end of the story, he buys the book by outbidding a representative of the Bibliothèque Nationale. In his search for the work he finds several manuscripts dealing with the Abbé's family, one of which, a sort of diary kept by Angélique de Longueville, the great-aunt of the Abbé, particularly intrigues him. Although many digressions intervene, the central part of *Angélique* is devoted to the adventures of this high-spirited girl of aristocratic family who falls in love with one La Corbière, son of a butcher and now in the service of Angélique's father, escapes with him from her watchful family, and eventually marries him in Italy. The story itself is Romanesque, almost a pastiche of an adventure novel, told now by Angélique, now by Nerval in the third person, with some final remarks on her later fortunes after her return to France by another member of the family. The story itself is rather banal, but Nerval was obviously attracted to it by the character of the heroine who becomes one of the *filles du feu* because of her great love for her often ungrateful and cruel husband.

Other elements in the work give it more interest. Nerval plays the role of bibliophile and, as such, makes some fascinating comments on the world of the bibliophile and his problems in the France of 1851. He is also concerned with censorship and especially with the Riancey amendment to the laws governing the press, an amendment directed "against any writing having the form of a novel and liable to a supplementary tax."[38] Nerval informs the reader that he is not a novelist, and throughout the work reiterates that he is interested in the historical rather than the Romanesque aspects of de Bucquoy.

The author's interests in French history—the Medicis, Henry IV and his mistress Gabrielle d'Este, in architecture, ruins, local landscapes, and especially those of the Valois, are all evidenced in *Angélique*. But the evocative magic that is found in *Sylvie* in Nerval's creation of a world of memory and imagination is lacking in this piece. Despite some Watteauesque descriptions of landscapes, *Angélique* is more the work of a narrator and observer than of one who feels and, in feeling, recreates an atmosphere, a place, a time. The work is personal and Gérard, not Angélique or the Abbé de Bucquoy, is the major character. He relates his impressions, his interests, his obsessions, and many anecdotes about his research. He is a rambler whose physical and mental peregrinations provide the real kernel of the story. His interest in local legends and popular songs, best evidenced in *Chansons et légendes du Valois,* is seen here, too. It might be noted in passing that Nerval was, of all the French Romantics, the one most interested in, and fond of, the legends and folk music of the countryside and especially of his native Valois. As such he is the predecessor of so many contemporary classical and popular musicians of all countries who have delved into their country's past in order to explain its culture. In the tone of a Barrès, Nerval writes in *Angélique*:

Whatever one might say philosophically we are held to the soil by many bonds. One doesn't sweep away the ashes of his ancestors from the soles of his shoes,—and the poorest keeps somewhere a sacred memory which reminds him of those who loved him. Whether it be religion or philosophy, everything indicates this eternal cult of memories to man.[39]

Nerval reveals in *Angélique* his fascination with the untutored and pure voice of the female with its innocence of expression:

Music in this country has not been spoiled by the imitation of Parisian operas, salon songs, or organ melodies. We are still at Senlis with the music of the sixteenth century, traditionally conserved since the Médicis.[40]

Purity in woman attracts Nerval, and when it leads to his falling in love, both the purity and love take on a mythical cast. Angélique notes in her manuscript that love is the queen of all passions, and Nerval in a note comments that "Love was feminine in gender in this epoch,"[41] a fact that explains its appeal to the poet for whom Woman was the Goddess. Writing of the warrior women of the early French tribes, Gérard remarks that, warriors or not, women never lost their sway in France either as queens or as favorites. His own mother, although not a warrior, had followed his father with the army and died in the war. This fact explains to a certain degree Nerval's interest in women like Angélique de Longueville.

Nerval seldom deals with subjects that do not have some personal meaning for him. He tends to see aspects of himself in historical characters. He writes of one of the de Bucquoys: "his face reveals imagination and energy with a slight tendency toward the whimsical. The Abbé de Bucquoy must have succeeded him as dreamers succeed men of action."[42] Or as Nerval the dreamer succeeded his father, the man of action.

A peculiar aspect of Nerval's art, and one of which he was

at least somewhat aware, is his reliance in his descriptions of landscapes, be they of the Valois or the Near East, on real paintings both as points of comparison or as actual subjects of description. He writes of autumn:

At this moment in spite of the morning mist we notice tableaux worthy of the great Flemish artists. In the châteaux and in the museums one still finds the spirit of the painters of the North. There are always points of view with rose or bluish tints in the sky, with trees half shedding their leaves, with fields in the distance or in the foreground of bucolic scenes. *The Voyage to Cythera* of Watteau was conceived in the transparent and colored mists of this country. It is a Cythera traced on a small island of these ponds created by the overflowings of the Oise and the Aisne, those rivers so calm and peaceful in summer.[43]

Angélique is a self-conscious work in the sense that Nerval is aware of his manipulations of form and content, and he is always in lucid control of the material in which he is the basic protagonist. This piece is basically intellectual, for the author is constantly reminding the reader of what he is doing and what he plans to do. In the seventh letter, for example, he writes:

Before speaking of the great resolution of Angélique de Longueville I ask permission to say one more word. Then I shall only rarely interrupt the narrative. Since it is forbidden to us to create an historical *novel* we are forced to serve the sauce on a different plate from the fish. That is to say the local descriptions, the feeling of the epoch, the analysis of characters—outside the materially true tales.[44]

This technique is reinforced at the end of the work in the section of the twelfth letter called "Reflexions":

"And then . . ." (It's thus that Diderot began a tale, I'll be told.)
"Go ahead!"
"You've imitated Diderot himself."
"Who had imitated Sterne . . ."
"Who had imitated Swift."
"Who had imitated Rabelais."
"Who had imitated Merlin Coccaïe . . ."
"Who had imitated Petronius . . ."
"Who had imitated Lucian. And Lucian had imitated many others . . .

Even if it was only the author of the *Odyssey* who moved his hero around the Mediterranean for ten years to bring him back at last to that fabulous Ithaca whose queen, surrounded by about fifty suitors, unraveled each night what she had woven during the day."

"But Ulysses ended by refinding Ithaca."

"And I refound the Abbé de Bucquoy."[45]

Angélique, then, does have a form even in its apparent form-lessness, and its technique is in the line of the works Nerval himself mentions above. Yet *Angélique,* despite its occasional charm and structural interest, is not one of Nerval's best works.

Sylvie, in contrast, is undoubtedly one of the writer's master-pieces and the most perfect work in *Les Filles du feu* from the point of view of interrelation of style and content. Like most of Nerval's later works, it is quasi-autobiographical and at times represents a good example of the artist's theory of the "overflow of the dream into real life."[46] In *Sylvie,* time and reality are often ambiguous, and the point of the work is missed if these two elements are not discussed.

Time exists on several levels in *Sylvie.* There is the moment when the author is writing the story (1852?) and the first episode which took place about a dozen years earlier. It is from this second base that the story begins and to which it returns from time to time in the course of the narrative, which is told in the first person. But there is also the time of memory, memory of a more distant past, the time of childhood which possesses some of the qualities of the dream.

The work, which is divided into fourteen chapters, begins with a section entitled "Nuit perdue," in which the narrator is leaving a theatre to which he comes almost every night for love of an actress and her voice. For a year he had not thought of finding out what she was because he "feared troubling the magic mirror which reflected her image for him."[47] As in many of his works that deal with his loves, Nerval declares that he "felt himself live in her, and she lived for (him)alone."[48] She is almost exclusively at the center of his private world which is his momentary reality. When he is writing in the present of this incident of the past, he discusses his epoch and especially its attitude toward love:

Love, alas!, vague forms, rose and blue tints, metaphysical phantoms! Seen up close the real woman revolted our ingenuity; she had to appear as queen or goddess and not be approached.[49]

This statement is one of the keys to this work as well as to other writings of Nerval, for love to him was platonic adoration created by the imagination, and it was soiled by or died from the reality of the goddess becoming a human female. Speaking of the actress, Nerval claims he was pursuing an image and nothing more. Since love in its various forms and the creation of myth about the women loved are the basic subjects of *Sylvie*, it is important that Nerval introduce them in the first chapter, for they will continue to appear throughout the work in various contrapuntal forms.

Leaving the theatre "with the bitter sadness that a vanished dream leaves,"[50] Nerval joins some friends for witty conversation and discovers that the actress's current suitor is sitting near him. He decides to return home and picks up a paper which contains an announcement of a Fête du Bouquet provincial. "Tomorrow the archers of Senlis are to return the bouquet to the archers of Loisy."[51] These words awaken in Nerval a new group of impressions, much as the taste of the madeleine did to the Narrator of Proust's *A la recherche du temps perdu*. "It was the memory of the province long forgotten, a distant echo of the simple festivals of youth."[52] He goes to bed but is unable to sleep, and, immersed in a half sleep, he begins to remember his youth. "That state in which the mind still resists the bizarre combinations of the dream often permits one to see compressed in a few minutes the most striking pictures of a long period of ones life."[53] Nerval proceeds to relate a childhood memory that took place in the Valois near a château of the epoch of Henry IV, one not unlike that of the poem "Fantaisie." Young girls were dancing and singing folk songs. Nerval had come with Sylvie, a peasant girl, but his attention was soon drawn to a beautiful blonde girl named Adrienne. Soon he is in the center of the dance with her and must therefore kiss her. In order to return to the dance she must sing a song, and she so enchants her audience with it that Nerval crowns her with a laurel wreath, and she soon disappears into the château.

But for the poet "she resembled Dante's Beatrice who smiled at the poet as he wandered on the edge of the eternal abodes."[54] Jealous, Sylvie wept over this incident and Nerval was helpless to do anything about it. Recalled to Paris for his studies, he took with him the double image "of a tender friendship sadly broken off,—then of an impossible and vague love that was the source of unhappy tears."[55] But the image of Adrienne remained triumphant, and only the next year did he discover that she had entered a convent.

In the third chapter, the poet is still in bed thinking of this incident of his youth:

Everything was explained to me by this half-dreamed memory. That vague and hopeless love, conceived for an actress, which overcame me every evening at the time of the performance and leaving me only when I went to sleep had its seed in the memory of Adrienne . . . The resemblance of a figure forgotten for many years was henceforth drawn with a singular preciseness. It was a pencil drawing blurred by time that had become a picture, like those old sketches of the masters you admire in a museum and then you find elsewhere the striking original.

To love a nun in the form of an actress! . . . and suppose it were the same person! It's enough to drive one insane! It is a fatal fascination in which the unknown attracts you like the will-o'-the-wisp fleeing over the rushes in still water . . . Let's get our foothold back in reality.[56]

Nerval is already in the process of creating a myth, of interweaving time periods, for the past has merged with and become the present.

Desiring to visit again the haunts of his childhood, he decides to go there immediately to catch the end of the festivities about which he had read in the newspaper. He hires a carriage for the four-hour trip and en route begins to remember the times he went so often to Loisy. Chapters 4-6 deal with these memories which are closer in time to the present he is narrating than to the scene of childhood when he crowned Adrienne. The time element remains constant in these three chapters: They all relate to a certain period in the past, a period of happiness with Sylvie in the rustic beauty of the Valois. But even in the almost Rousseauesque description of rustic pleasures, dances, walks,

festivals with their idyllic overtones, the memory of Adrienne
haunts the Narrator who, having escorted Sylvie home from a
dance, is wandering near the convent of Saint S . . . and wondering if that was the one that Adrienne had joined. He wanted
to look over the walls but restrained himself as from a profa-
nation. By this time period Adrienne had already become associated with the goddess, the untouchable.

On returning to Sylvie's house, Nerval and she decide to
visit her aunt at Othys. Once there, Sylvie decides to don her
aunt's wedding dress and says, "Ah! I'm going to look like an
old fairy."[57] Nerval thinks to himself of the eternally young fairy
of legends.[58] Nerval himself dresses in Sylvie's uncle's wedding
suit and, in their finery, they dine with her aunt. He remarks,
"We were husband and wife for a whole beautiful summer
morning."[59]

In Chapter 7, the time changes abruptly back to that of the
carriage ride to Loisy, and Nerval then recounts another memory of the countryside at an indefinite time in the past. It
relates to a soirée that he "crashed" with Sylvie's brother, but
the reality of part of the memory is confusing, even doubtful
to him. On stage were a group of girls performing what
seemed to be a mystery play of old:

Each voice sang one of the splendours of this extinguished globe, and
the angel of death defined the causes of its destruction. A spirit came
up from the abyss, holding the flaming sword in her hand and con-
voked the others to come admire the glory of Christ, conqueror of
Hell. This spirit was Adrienne transfigured by her costume as she was
already by her vocation. The nimbus of gilt cardboard around her
angelic head appeared quite naturally to us as a circle of light. Her
voice had grown stronger and greater in range, and the endless
fioriture of Italian song embroidered the severe phrases of a stately
recitative with the trills of birds.[60]

But Nerval wonders if these details were real or whether he
dreamed them. He distinctly remembers certain aspects of the
evening, yet he is not sure that the apparition of Adrienne took
place. Here is another example of the overflowing of the dream
into the real world, for Adrienne, the creature of dream, has
through a process of mythologization become as real to the

author as anyone still alive and known to him. The dream thus becomes reality and may take precedence over quotidian reality because the author chooses that it do so. Yet although this super-reality exists in the present, the fact that its origin may be doubtful, even to the author, is of minor importance.

At the beginning of Chapter 8 Nerval returns to the action of a dozen or so years before and tells of his arrival at the Ball at Loisy. There he refinds Sylvie whom he calls a nymph of olden days as he escorts her home from the party. From Chapters 8 to 12 the time period remains the same—the period following his arrival at Loisy. The past, however, still holds him in its power, for Nerval is torn between the reality of Sylvie who loves him and the claims of Adrienne whose presence he constantly feels. On returning from the ball he throws himself to his knees and asks Sylvie to save him because he has returned to her forever. But being the fairy rather than the saint, she is powerless to help him.

Wandering by himself in Rousseau's Ermenonville, Nerval is reminded of Sylvie: "The enchanting gaze of Sylvie, her wild running, her joyous cries formerly gave so much charm to the places I had just gone through."[61] But Sylvie had changed: She had read a good deal, Rousseau and Scott among others, and her innocence seemed to have been tampered with by civilization or perhaps by proximity to Nerval. She no longer wants to sing folk songs but rather operatic airs and, as Nerval underscores, she *phrased*. Sylvie is no longer the mythical creature she once was, no longer a nymph of the Valois, but a modern young woman. In an aside the author, writing in 1853, asks:

Do women really feel that such and such a word passes through the lips without coming from the heart? One would not believe so, seeing that they are so easily deceived, noting the choices they most often make: there are some men who play the comedy of love so well! I have never been able to do so even though I knew that certain women knowingly accept being deceived. Besides, there is something sacred about a love that goes back to childhood . . .[62]

Sylvie was now for him a sister whom he could not seduce.

In Chapter 13 he returns to Paris, and time is accelerated as he leaves a note for Aurélie, the actress, and then goes to

Germany. Months pass during which he writes a play and then decides to return to France where Aurélie accepts the leading role in his drama. She does not believe that Nerval loves her and points out an aging actor of leading romantic roles as the one who does.

Three loves have been lost in the course of the narrative: Adrienne, Sylvie, Aurélia. Nerval writes of this in the last chapter:

Such are the chimeras which charm and beguile us in the morning of life. I have tried to set them down without much order, but many hearts will understand me. Illusions fall one after the other like the rinds of fruit, and the fruit is experience. Its taste is bitter yet there is something that fortifies in its sharpness . . .[63]

In the Valois he has lost Adrienne and Sylvie, two halves of a single love: "The one was the sublime ideal, the other the gentle reality."[64] In Paris he has lost Aurélie, a woman who has traits of the other two. Nerval has relived his past experiences, and thus they have become a part of the present of the man writing the story. But they seem more alive than the present itself, and the work ends with another memory. Nerval asked Sylvie one day at Dammartin, where Aurélie was acting, if the actress did not resemble Adrienne. Sylvie laughed and then, as if reproaching herself, told the Narrator that Adrienne had died at the convent of Saint-S . . . in 1832.

Sylvie ends on this note, but, in reality, the ending is not sad. Adrienne is in certain ways reincarnated in Aurélie. The past never dies; it is always present in memory or in dreams. Reality, thus, is basically subjective, the product of our looking at the worlds of time and seeing them as coexistent. The realistic details of the memory are important for they have been chosen unconsciously by the mind to the exclusion of others because they are based on experienced emotions. Thus the superfluous details tend to fall aside, and Nerval's reality becomes that of the dreamer-lover rather than that of the chronicler. *Sylvie* is a masterpiece of poetic analysis of time and the realities existent within it. Not until Rimbaud, Proust, and the Surrealists is the personal, dreamlike, subjective world so well explored. The "outpouring of dream into real life" that is mentioned in *Aurélia* finds its first major incarnation in *Sylvie*. But it is neither the dream world nor the real world that is more important: It is the combination of the two, the outpouring of one into the other, and their ultimate combination produces a sort of super-reality that emotionally suggests more than it rationally tells.

The basic setting of *Sylvie* is pastoral—the country of the Valois, and in this country, beginning with Nerval's trip from Paris to the final paragraph in which all three loves are united at the performance at Dammartin, we follow, over various time periods, the sentimental journey of the Narrator. There is no attempt at objectivity here and no need for it. The characters, other than the Narrator, are, of necessity, seen through his eyes, but they are seen through a sort of magification. Aurélie is bathed in the light of the stage. She is a magic and almost inaccessible creature whom the Narrator would seem to prefer to worship from afar rather than to know, for the knowledge of her, when he does receive it from her own lips, takes away the magic qualities of her character. Adrienne is seen in the light of religion and is as unobtainable, except in reverie, as Aurélie. Sylvie, too, is magified; she is the nymph of the Valois, characterized more realistically than the other two loves, but still the product of Nerval's subjective viewpoint. The other characters, minor all, serve only as colorful puppets in the poet's sentimental excursions. Once again it is Nerval himself who is the major character and unifying force of the work. Yet in the character of Nerval the Narrator, the only unity is the subjectivity of his approach on each of the time levels already discussed. Everyone including himself is seen through and by him. Sometimes the Nerval of the present comments on the other Nervals; mostly he becomes them through his reveries, through his reliving of past times in the present.

Even the atmosphere of the Valois is presented subjectively. The fields and streams, woods and houses, the châteaux and local landmarks are presented more for their emotional value than for the realism of their actuality. The Nature of Nerval's world is a magic one, not that of the German writers or even of Rousseau whom Nerval almost consciously imitates in several sections of this work. It is a seen world almost as Watteau had

painted it. (Watteau was from the Valois, and it is no coincidence that Chapter 6 is titled "Un Voyage à Cythère.") It is
poetically alive because of its sentimental connotations. Thus
the décor and the narrative sections themselves provide a unity
of tone, a sort of theatrical magic in which Nerval is director,
scenic designer, and star. The world he creates becomes momentarily real, as any good stage performance does, and later an
atmosphere lingers, a haunting quality from which it is difficult
to escape. The reader is left with impressions of impressions, but,
as Nerval knew, the heart understands.

Although not of the quality of *Sylvie*, *Octavie* is one of the
most important stories in *Les Filles du feu*. In this short narrative, told in the first person, are found the sources of many of
the allusions in his later works as well as his tendency to mythol-
ogize both the events and people of his life. Probably through
the process of memory, a young English girl acquires in this
narrative the characteristics of the ideal beloved, and the whole
Neapolitan interlude in Nerval's life takes on the quality of
myth. It must be noted that references to this period abound
in *Les Chimères*.

Nerval relates that in the spring of 1835 he experienced a
strong desire to see Italy and left Paris to find distraction from
a fatal love affair. While in Marseilles he encounters an English
girl who is traveling with her sick father. Like him, this "daughter of the waters," named Octavie, swims every day. One day she
gives him a fish she has caught, and he is amused by the present.
Soon the mythologization takes place, for Nerval relates Octavie
to the Siren and the Ondine. Because of an outbreak of cholera
in Marseilles, Nerval takes the land route to Civita Vecchia
where he again meets Octavie, this time at the theatre. Fate
seems determined that they meet the next day on the boat to
Naples, and she makes an appointment to meet him in Portici.
When she makes the date she playfully menaces him with a
gold-headed cane, which, like the fish, seems to have the value
of a talisman as well as strong sexual overtones.

When Nerval arrives in Naples, he finds an old acquaintance
who invites him to have tea with his family. After an enjoyable
philosophical discussion with his friend's sisters, he leaves and
experiences a strange adventure which he describes in a letter

he wrote later, in 1838, to the one he loved and left in Paris in
1835. The letter deals with his state of mind during the two
time periods—1838 and 1835 when he had the adventure in
Naples. His mental state at the time of writing the letter is
one of an almost morbid anxiety for he relates that he has
experienced a fatal premonition. Because his relationship with
Jenny Colon (Aurélie) is troublesome, he writes her that his
greatest desire is to die for her. At the age of thirty, death,
which had obsessed him for several years, acquired the fascination that it held for him for the rest of his life:

Die, good God! Why does that idea recur to me constantly as if there
were only my death which was the equivalent of the happiness you
promise? Death! This word does not give out anything somber in
my thoughts. It appears to me crowned with pale roses, as at the end
of a festival. I have sometimes dreamed that smiling it waited for
me at the headboard of the bed of an adored woman after ecstasy,
after happiness, and that it said to me, "Come on, young man!, you've
had your whole share of joy in this world. Come, sleep now. Come,
rest in my arms. I am not beautiful, but I am good and willing to
help, and I don't give pleasure but rather eternal calm."[65]

The theme of love and death, of love in death and death in
love, and the irreconcilability of the two in this life joins in
Octavie the themes of guilt and purity, guilt about sex which
betrays an ideal, and woman as the pure ideal of platonic love.
In the letter Nerval continues by relating that the same image
of death, experienced in 1838, already presented itself to him
in Naples three years before. There, upon leaving his friend's
home and having lost his way, he came across a young seamstress
who resembled the woman to whom he is writing the letter. He
accompanied her home and then imagined the young Italian to
be his French love. But even this encounter had mystic connotations for the young poet:

The room that I entered had something mystic about it by chance
or the singular choice of the objects it contained.[66]

There was a black madonna covered with cheap finery and a
figure of St. Rosalie crowned with violet roses.[67] The walls were

decorated with old pictures of the four elements representing mythological divinities. On a table was a treatise on divination and dreams which made him think of his companion as some sort of sorceress or at least a gypsy.[68] The girl began to speak a language which he did not understand and had never heard. She dressed herself in false finery, which caused Nerval to have odd sensations:

... and I, little accustomed to the burning wines of Vesuvius, felt objects turn before my eyes. This woman with the strange manners, royally garbed, proud and capricious, appeared to me as one of those female magicians of Thessaly to whom one gave one's soul for a dream.[69]

After apparently having had sexual relations with her, he leaves the seamstress and begins to climb Posilipo above the grotto. He is excited by the natural beauty, but in his mind is the idea of death:

O Gods! I don't know what profound sadness dwelt in my heart, but it was nothing other than the cruel thought that I was not loved. I had seen what might be the ghost of happiness; I had used up all the gifts of God; I was under the most beautiful sky in the world in the presence of the most perfect nature ... but at four hundred leagues from the only woman who existed for me and who even ignored my existence. Not being loved and having no hope of ever being loved![70]

Nerval attempted suicide, but was restrained by the idea of the rendezvous with Octavie, which made his fatal ideas disappear. He keeps the appointment with Octavie and her father and takes her to the Temple of Isis at Pompeii where she plays Isis and he Osiris, whose divine mysteries he explains. But he feels he is not worthy of Octavie's love. In his mind she has become the goddess, the unapproachable one, whereas the seamstress is the magician, or, as he puts it in "El Desdichado" Octavie is the saint and the seamstress the fairy.[71] Again Nerval makes the contrast between the mystic and the magic.

Ten years later he returned to Naples and found Octavie, who had married a young painter who is completely paralyzed. But Nerval claims that Octavie has kept the secret of happiness:

The boat which brought me back to Marseilles carried the memory of this beloved apparition like a dream, and I said to myself that perhaps I had left happiness there. Octavie had kept the secret with her.[72]

This experience, memories of which recur frequently in Nerval's writings, was undoubtedly one of the most imporant of his life. Perhaps only a banal moment of happiness, it became transformed into a situation of mystical importance and took a major place in Nerval's personal mythology. Octavie joins Adrienne and Aurélia in Nerval's category of saints. She is, as were the Adrienne and Jenny Colon characters, based on temporal reality, but has been transformed into the mystical reality of the poet's imagination.

In this brief semiautobiographical story (certain details are not accurate or have been changed for various reasons),[73] Nerval presents, as in *Sylvie* and *Aurélia*, a character who remains a wraith because she has become disembodied in the original sense of the word. Thus, the main character once again is Nerval himself. The other characters, including the seamstress, have no reality of their own. They are seen as refracted from the mind of the author and as such have symbolical but little fictional value. Their reality is in Nerval, and in *Octavie*, as in most of the other prose works, his reality (be it a superreality or his own temporal reality) is the only meaningful thing. In *Octavie* it becomes more and more obvious that Nerval, perhaps unwittingly, is the subject of his own work, that he is, of all the Romantic authors, the one whose self (fragmented though it may be) is not only the subject of his works, but the supernatural mirror through which the rest of the world is seen.

Isis is the best introduction to Nerval's concept of syncretism. Unlike the other sections that make up *Les Filles du feu, Isis* is not based on Nerval's experiences with a living or historical woman, but rather on the cult of the Egyptian goddess whose temple at Pompeii so fascinated the writer. The work, parts of which are based on a German source,[74] is a description of the temple, its origins as a factor in the religious life of the Roman empire, and a reconstruction of the rites practiced there. This bit of historical reconstruction is interesting, but it pales before

the exposition of the religious concepts of Nerval which are
lucidly presented.

Nerval sees that the cult of Isis was partly influential because
of the human need for the marvelous and the prevalence of
human superstition in the ancient world.

All that the strange ceremonies and mysteries of the Cabires and of
the gods of Eleusis, of Greece, all that the bacchanales of the *Liber
Pater* and the *Hébon* of Campania had offered separately to the
passion for the marvelous and to superstition itself was, through a
religious artifice, gathered together in the secret cult of the Egyptian
goddess, as in a subterranean canal which receives water from a
crowd of tributaries.[75]

Nerval claims that in all epochs gods had to conform to the
customs of men, so the Temple of Isis at Pompeii was known
for its sexual license:

But these are excesses common to all cults in their epochs of decadence.
The same accusations were addressed to the mysterious practices and
agapes of the first Christians. The idea of a *holy land* in which the
memory of original traditions and a sort of filial adoration were to
be joined together for all people, of a holy water fit for the consecra-
tions and purifications of the faithful, presents nobler links between
the two cults . . . of which one has, so to say, served as transition to
the other.[76]

Christianity is seen as a cult, like any other, and the resemblance
between it and other religions of antiquity are analyzed by
Nerval almost in the manner of writers of contemporary studies
of comparative religion. Isis, for example, as Nerval points out,
could not be honored without Osiris. He writes, "The faithful
even believed in the real presence of Osiris in the water of the
Nile."[77] As in Christianity, a form of divine transubstantiation
is found in the Egyptian religion.

In the third part of the essay, which is divided into four
sections, Nerval becomes personal, begins to describe his own
experiences, and recounts that after his trip to the Near East,
on a second visit to the Temple of Isis he had had a near
religious experience:

While contemplating those two stars that had been long adored in this temple under the names of Osiris and Isis and under the mystic attributes alluding to their different phases, I sat down on a rock and felt myself caught by a strong emotion. Child of a century skeptical rather than unbelieving, hesitating between two contrary educations—that of the Revolution which denied all and that of social reaction which claims to bring back all of the Christian beliefs—would I see myself forced to believe everything as our fathers the philosophers had been to deny everything? I thought of that magnificent preamble to the *Ruines* of Volney which makes the Genius of the past appear on the ruins of Palmyra, and which borrows from such high inspirations only the power of destroying bit by bit all of the religious traditions of the human race. Thus, beneath the effort of modern reason, Christ himself perished, Christ the most recent of the revealers who, in the name of a higher reason had formerly depopulated the heavens. O nature! O eternal mother! was that really the fate reserved for the last of your celestial sons? Have mortals come to repulse all hope and all prestige, and, raising your sacred veil, goddess of Saïs, did the most devoted of your followers find himself therefore face to face with the image of Death?

If the successive fall of beliefs led to that result would it be more consoling to fall into the contrary excess and try to take up again the illusions of the past?[78]

In this quotation Nerval poses a question which preoccupied him intellectually throughout his life, one which, in his periods of exaltation and madness, became all-absorbing. When he was mentally stable, as he most likely was when writing this essay, he was aware of the unsolvable conflict between rationalism and religion, but in his periods of madness or surreal states of mind (such as in his writing of many of the *Chimères* and parts of *Aurélia*) he found his solace and often his despair in religious syncretism.

The fourth part deals essentially with aspects of this religious syncretism. Nerval finds that paganism had acquired new strength from its Egyptian origin and tended to bring back more and more the diverse mythological conceptions to the principle of unity. He writes, "That eternal Nature ... (which) Apulius freely calls Isis is the name which for him sums up all the others. It is the primitive identity of this queen of heaven with different attributes, with the changing mask."[79] Isis thus becomes in her various guises Cybèle, Minerva, the Paphian Venus, the Dictynne Diana, Proserpine, Ceres, Juno, Bellona, Hecate, and Nemesis, but her real name is Isis, as she informed Lucius. She also told him that he must consecrate the rest of his life to her and even adore her "... in the shades of the Acheron or in the Elysian Fields."[80] She said to him, "... and if by the observance of my cult and by an inviolate chastity you merit well of me you will know that I alone can prolong your spiritual life beyond its marked limits."[81] The influence of his readings on Nerval can be seen here, for the concept of chastity, the adoration of the goddess, and the feeling of guilt for even trivial amorous dalliances are all found in this quotation which is an adaptation of a passage from the *Metamorphoses* of Apulius.

Nerval sees the Virgin Mary as the modern parallel of Isis, the chaste mother, and finds the roots of Christianity in the Egyptian religion:

Certainly, if paganism had always manifested such a pure conception of the divinity, the religious principles that issued from the old land of Egypt would still reign, according to that form, over modern civilization. But isn't it to be noticed that it is also from Egypt that the first foundations of the Christian faith come? Orpheus and Moses, both initiated into the mysteries of Isis, simply announced sublime truth to different races, truths that the difference of customs, of language and space of time little by little then altered or transformed entirely.[82]

But time is repeating itself:

Today it seems that Catholicism itself varying according to countries, has undergone a reaction analagous to that which took place in the last years of polytheism. In Italy, Poland, Greece, Spain, in all the peoples sincerely attached to the Roman Church, hasn't the devotion to the Virgin become a sort of exclusive cult? Isn't it still the holy Mother, holding in her arms the saviour and mediator child, who dominates minds? And whose apparition still produces conversions similar to that of the hero of Apulius? Isis does not have only either the child in her arms or the cross in her hand like the Virgin: the same zodiacal sign is consecrated to them; the moon is under their feet; the same halo shines around their heads ...[83]

Nerval wonders if in all intelligent cults there isn't certain divine revelation. Even in early Christianity oracles were invoked. However, the crux of the matter, and it is developed most completely in *Aurélia*, is that Christianity eventually forbade all other religions. Because of this attitude, Nerval feels that much was lost to the world. When he thinks of himself as a Cainite and attacks the Christian God, he is annoyed because he has tried to expand his horizon of knowledge and experience, a thing forbidden by the Church. He writes sensibly, "A new evolution of dogmas could, on certain points, make the religious testimonies of different times agree. It would be so fine to absolve the heroes and wise men of antiquity and rip them from eternal maledictions."[84]

Each religion borrows from preceding ones and, for a time, respects certain practices that it tries to make harmonize with its own dogmas. But the concept found in many religions that intrigues Nerval most is that of the Mother and the Redeemer:

Is the child Horus, suckled by the divine mother, and who will be the *Word* (logos) of future ages, the *Redeemer* promised to the earth and long predicted by poets and oracles? Is it the Iacchus-Iesus of the mysteries of Eleusis . . . springing forth from the arms of Demeter, the *pantheistic* goddess? Or rather isn't it true that one must reunite all these different modes of a single idea and that it was always an admirable theogonic thought to present for the adoration of men a celestial Mother whose child is the hope of the world?[85]

Christ is equated with Osiris, Adonis, Atys, the murdered god, the fertility god who is resurrected in the springtime on the third day when the bloodied corpse has disappeared and the immortal god has been revealed. A woman made divine, be she mother, wife, or lover, always weeps over the corpse, "victim of a hostile principle which triumphs by his death, but which will one day be conquered."[86] Nerval finds the ancient religions ones of hope, serenity, and joy, the products of a prosperous and happy people. But in Rome Christianity, a religion of grief and despair, took over:

Philosophy accomplished, on the other hand, a work of assimilation and moral unity; the thing waited for by men came true in the order of events. This divine Mother, this Saviour, that a sort of prophetic mirage had announced here and there from one end of the world to the other finally appeared as the full day which succeeds the vague glimmers of dawn.[87]

Isis is a capital work for the understanding of the most hermetic of the *Chimères,* of *Aurélia,* and of Nerval's religious concepts in general, for these ideas penetrate most aspects of his work. That he became the figures of his religious myths in his periods of madness not only lends poignancy to his life, but explains much of the hermeticism of his work.

The only piece in dramatic form in *Les Filles de feu, Corilla,* is called a proverb, and it resembles in some ways the proverbs of Alfred de Musset. The play takes place on a street near the opera house of Naples. Fabio, poet, musician, and double of Nerval, speaks with Mazetto, an employee of the theatre, about his prospects with the famous soprano, Corilla, with whom he is in love. Mazetto informs him that she will soon appear and make a rendezvous with him. A woman does appear and makes an appointment for five o'clock. Another suitor of Corilla comes on stage and tells Fabio that she has just told him she would meet him at another place at five o'clock. Neither believing the other, the two men quarrel, for each is convinced that Corilla is incapable of such duplicity. Agreeing to duel the following morning, Marcelli leaves for the rendezvous and soon again appears with Corilla on his arm. Fabio surprises them, but Corilla claims she has never heard of Fabio nor received his gifts or letters. Mazetto then enters and explains that he has never given them to her because he has also been the intermediary for Marcelli whose letters he *has* given to the singer. He arranged for a woman who resembles Corilla to meet Fabio because he is a poet and lives in a world of unreality. Corilla leaves with Marcelli, and Fabio, alone, bemoans his fate. Suddenly the Bouquetière appears and tries to console him, but he thinks only of his ideal whom he does not recognize in her disguise until she sings for him. Marcelli enters, and Corilla tells Fabio he loves his image of her on stage too much, and then tells Marcelli that he loves himself too much. The three go off to dine together as the curtain falls.

To all appearances *Corilla* is a simple story about two men and their rivalry for what appears to be a capricious but beautiful and talented woman. However, the characterization of Fabio is more complex than the story would suggest. He may not be an exact duplicate of Nerval, but he does exhibit many of his creator's traits. In fact, *Corilla* gives the impression of being a play in which Nerval is observing himself, his weakness in love, his insecurity, his fear of being rebuffed, his realization that it is only the ideal he loves and not the reality. Corilla, when she is performing on stage, is a goddess for him, but the realization that she is also a human being destroys Fabio's illusions. Even before he meets her he is apprehensive about the meeting:

I am going to see her! . . . A word from her will realize my dream or make it disappear forever! Ah! I'm afraid of risking here more than I can gain; my passion was great and pure and brushed the world without touching it. She lived only in radiant palaces and on enchanted shores. Here she is brought back to earth and forced to walk like all the others. Like Pygmalion I adored the exterior form of a woman; only the statue moved every evening with a divine grace before my eyes, and from her mouth only pearls of melody fell. And now here she is coming down to me. But love which caused this miracle is a shameful valet of comedy, and the ray which makes this adored idol live for me is of those that Jupiter poured on the breast of Danae.[88]

If hope is in Fabio's heart, the happiness found there is not joyous. "Happiness makes me sad; it forces me to think of the unhappiness which always closely follows it."[89] Fear of the unknown, of something over which he has no control, especially his emotions and contradictory heart and states of mind make Fabio one of those people incapable of action, one suited only for dreams.

Nerval's obsession with the double is evidenced in this work by the flower girl impersonating Corilla and then Corilla herself impersonating the flower girl. Fabio is annoyed with himself for failing to recognize the false Corilla to be such, but he is hardly more able to distinguish Corilla from the flower girl she is playing. Speaking to Corilla in her disguise, he says:

You are the wild flower of the fields; but who could mistake you two for each other? You undoubtedly remind me of some of her characteristics, and your heart is worth more than hers, perhaps. But who can replace in the soul of a lover the beautiful image that every day he has taken pleasure in adorning with a new prestige? The latter no longer exists in reality on the earth; she is engraved only at the bottom of the faithful heart, and no portrait will ever be able to render her imperishable beauty.[90]

The world of fantasy is killed by the real world when it becomes part of it. Corilla says, "(Fabio) adores in me only the actress, perhaps, and his love needs distance and the lighted footlights."

Fabio, then, has many of the characteristics of the Romantic hero in love, but he lacks the drive of the Hernanis and resembles more closely the cerebral heroes such as Adolphe and Chatterton. The portrait is psychologically sound and thus the character acquires elements of the universal. The other personages are secondary to Fabio. The scheming Mazetto and the egotistical Marcelli are types of no great originality. Corilla has, as do most of Nerval's women, a sort of ineffable charm, but we, like Fabio, see her as artist-goddess as well as a capricious earthly woman. She is basically a symbol for the dichotomy of the real and the ideal in Nerval's mind. What is uncommon about her presentation is that she visibly exists on the two levels. In *Corilla* Nerval presents lucidly and charmingly his basic relationship with both woman and goddess, a relationship demonstrated not quite so rationally but far more suggestively in *Aurélia*.

La Pandora (1854) was originally designed to be included in *Les Filles du feu*, but was not completed in time for publication in that work. The piece is a brief and often confused appendage to the section of *Voyage en Orient* entitled "Les Amours de Vienne," a sort of memoir of certain incidents that occurred either in reality or in reverie during his stay in Vienna. *La Pandora*, a short and haphazardly organized work, consists of memoirs of adventures, descriptions of receptions, a letter to Gautier, and the recounting of a mythological dream that is a forerunner of the many dreams in *Aurélia*. The myths of Prometheus and Pandora are used to express woman's duality and man's suffering in love. In Greek mythology Pandora was a woman created by Hephaestus, god of fire, and she was sent by

Zeus to punish Epimetheus, brother of Prometheus, for his kindness to man. Zeus gave her a box which he forbade her to open, but her curiosity caused her to disobey the god, and from the box came all man's troubles and sicknesses. Only hope remained inside. All mankind and Epimetheus, whom she had married, thus became her victims.

In *La Pandora* love is seen as suffering as well, perhaps, as a test. Nerval had met Marie Pleyel, a French pianist, in Vienna in 1839. He became enamored of her, and she serves as the model for the guileful Pandora. Based on personal experience that, for fictional purposes, may well have been exaggerated, *La Pandora* is substantially the story of Nerval's love which had left him, and others, with "cruel and sweet memories." Although the character Pandora never comes to life in the work, she does attain mythic status, for it is she who has caused Nerval/Prometheus all his sufferings. The writer thus thinks of himself and his problems in terms of myth and attempts to universalize his passion. After having left La Pandora in Vienna, he meets her a year later in a cold northern city:

My carriage stopped suddenly in the middle of the large square, and a divine smile nailed me strengthless to the ground. "There you are again, enchantress," I cried, "What have you done with the fatal box?"

"I filled it for you," she said, "with the most beautiful toys in Nuremberg. Won't you come admire them?"

But I began to run as fast as I could towards the Place de la Monnaie.

"O son of the gods, father of men!" she cried, "Stop a little. Today is Saint Sylvester's Day like last year . . . Where did you hide the fire of heaven that you stole from Jupiter?"

I did not want to answer: the name of Prometheus still displeases me a good deal, for I still feel in my side the eternal beak of the vulture from which Alcides freed me.

O Jupiter, when will my punishment end?[91]

The final cry of desperation comes from the hell in which Nerval is awaiting redemption, but in *La Pandora* there is no redemption. That will be found only in *Aurélia.*

The epigraph of *La Pandora* is a quotation from Goethe's *Faust,* and it shows Nerval's spiritual Manichaeism:

Two souls, alas, partook of my breast, and each of them wants to separate itself from the other. One, ardent with love, is attached to the world by means of the bodily organs. A supernatural movement draws the other far from the shadows towards the lofty abodes of our ancestors.[92]

The duality expressed in this quotation is developed at greater length and more brilliantly in *Aurélia*.

IV   *Quest, Dreams and Transcendence*

Generally considered to be the prose masterpiece of Nerval, *Aurélia* is a work unique in nineteenth-century French literature. The product at once of a visionary tainted by madness and a scrupulous artist, *Aurélia* is remarkable both in form and in the treatment of subject matter which describes literally and Romanesquely Nerval's states of mind over a period of fourteen years. The work, however, contains far more than a description of his personal tragedies, for it is an amazing recreation of a complex mind coping with the problems of life, death, guilt, love, suicide, reality, illusion, and religion.

As Nerval mentions in the first chapter, *Aurélia* is to be a sort of *Vita Nuova*,[93] and in the second part he claims it is a story similar to that of Orpheus returning from the underworld. Yet the piece is less optimistic than Dante's and less pessimistic than the story of the Thracian poet. It is a highly personal account of a quest and, as such, must be classified with the great works of quest of Western literature. But the quest is not basically for the father or the mother (although some psychoanalytical critics claim it is so)[94] or for the ultimate secret of life in general. It is rather a quest for self—the self as revealed by the conscious aspects of everyday life as well as by the world of dreams, the insistent memories of an often romanticized past, and of the esoterical mystical works that Nerval had read since his childhood. The quest for self is also a quest for salvation, but the means and aim of the salvation are not clarified until the second part, as Nerval alternates in his personal odyssey between states of the most profound despair and others of almost ecstatic hope. The way to salvation, in both a personal and mystical sense, is discovered in a tentative way by the end of the work, and the final mood is one of acceptance rather than of revelation.

The title character is not really a character in a fictional sense, but rather a wraith who is the cause of, or stimulus to, the poet's guilt and despair, and who mystically shows him the way to salvation. Aurélia, a name sounding similar to Laura, although the latter is derived from laurel, the crown of poets, the former from the dawn, is based on Jenny Colon, but the character of Jenny/Aurélia, vivid as it is to Nerval the narrator, is more symbolic to the reader. It is her presence or absence that dominates the poet's psyche throughout the work, but it is the narrator (Nerval) in whom both the author and reader are most interested. In *Aurélia* Nerval creates a great fictional character of himself (despite, or perhaps because of, the autobiographical elements in the work) as he journeys from darkness to a form of light. This is evidenced by the work itself, which is divided into two parts: Nerval's descent into madness and his gradual but always tenuous recovery from it.

The first chapter states that the dream is a second life, but there is an intermediate state between the dream and reality, for in the first moments of sleep the precise instant in which the self in another form continues the work of existence cannot be determined. "It is a dim tunnel which little by little becomes clearer."[95] In this state, the characters appear to be in a sort of limbo, but then a new light illuminates them as the world of Spirits opens up. At that moment one has moved completely from one reality to another. Nerval's models for these descriptions of the human soul are Swedenborg, Dante, and Apulius, and his object, in their manner, "is to transcribe the impressions of a long sickness which took place entirely in the mysteries of (his) own mind."[96] Whether this is Nerval's ultimate object becomes less clear in the subsequent sections of *Aurélia*, for he is describing these impressions on one level and is interpreting them on yet another. The writer himself raises an element of doubt bcause he is not sure that he experienced a mental sickness: he relates that he seemed to know and understand everything while he was in that condition, and thus experienced infinite delights. These ecstatic moments, however, proved to be of a purely transitory nature.

This *vita nuova* had two phases. The first deals with a remembered Aurélia (an idealized Jenny promoted to the rank of Beatrice and Laura) and a possibly platonic love between her and Nerval. In despair after their relationship, the sexual nature of which is never clearly delineated in this work, or in his letters for that matter, has been ruptured, Nerval notes that he had to decide whether to live or die. He chose life. Yet he was obsessed by a sense of guilt for a fault (which is never explicitly disclosed) for which there was no longer any pardon. This theme of guilt and consequent damnation which is found throughout the work is forcefully presented from the earliest pages. To mitigate the effects of the guilt, he threw himself into worldly life, but sometime later, while in Brussels, he again met Aurélia whom he still loved hopelessly. Sensing that she had pardoned him, he felt something of a religious nature mixed with his profane love. He had to go back to Paris on business, however, but planned to return to the Belgian capital. Until this point the narrative is basically realistic and deals with events that actually occurred. But then another world—one of hallucination, which for Nerval is just as real as everyday reality—is described. The shift from reality to premonition to hallucination is artfully accomplished, and it is evident that different modes of awareness exist on the same level for the author.

On returning home about midnight, he noticed the number of a house lighted by a street lamp and remarked that the number was thirty-three, his own age and Jenny Colon's. Thirty-three is a number with special connotations because Nerval knew that Christ and Alexander the Great had both died at that age. At the moment he noticed the number, he saw before him a woman who resembled Aurélia and said, "It's *her death* or mine that is announced to me."[97] He felt it was the latter, however, and that it would take place the next night at the same hour. That very night he had a dream that confirmed this idea. The dream is the first of many to be recounted in the book, and since it appears within what seems to be a lucid narration it makes a special impact. The poet saw himself wandering in a large building of several rooms. He stopped in one and believed he recognized his former teachers and fellow students. In another he chatted a bit, then left for his room in a hostelry which had immense stairs filled with busy travelers. Several times he became lost in the corridors and then he was suddenly struck by an androgynous being of abnormal size flying in space and unable to escape from the room. The being fell, and Nerval claims it was the Angel of Melancholia of Dürer. He screamed with fear and awakened.

This dream is of major import for an understanding of the book as a whole. As in most of his dreams, Nerval is wandering in spacious rooms. Places seem larger than life as does the non-human androgynous figure who is perhaps representative of pre-Adamite humanity. In dreams time spans are superimposed on each other, and thus his schooldays, his later viewing of the *Melancholia*, his readings of mystical works throughout his life are all intimately related in the dream. Several of the major themes that are developed in *Aurélia* are found in this dream: his personal past (teachers and students), the past of humanity (pre-Adamite), his sense of loss in space but not in time, for he is aware of different time periods simultaneously, his obsession with purity as represented by pre-Adamite humanity (a race that existed before sin entered the world in the person of Adam), his own guilt and premonitions of death. The fact that the first part of *Aurélia* deals with excursions via dreams or delirium into Nerval's ancestral past and then into the origins of humanity is clearly indicated by this dream, which also presages a sort of death to his rational existence in favor of another life, that of dreams.

Nerval then relates the circumstances of his first attack of madness. Following a star which he was convinced would influence his fate until the moment death should strike,[98] he suddenly noticed that his companion Paul, who has been accompanying him on a walk the next day, had grown larger and taken on the features of an apostle.[99] But he disappeared, and Nerval immediately found himself on a hill surrounded by a vast solitude. The scene was the setting for the combat of two Spirits and, the author says, resembled a biblical temptation. But Nerval refuses "your heaven" (Christianity) because he belongs to the Star which is anterior to Christianity and wants to go join his beloved and his friends there. Thus begins the spiritual conflict between Nerval's syncretism and Christianity

that is found throughout the whole work. It might be noted
that as Nerval's sense of place loses meaning and contours,
religious imagery comes into evidence.

But this scene, whether it actually happened or not, is most
important, for Nerval has not been relating a dream he had at
night. He calls what has happened "the pouring out of the
dream into real life," for henceforth everything will take on
a double aspect "without the power of reason ever lacking logic,
without memory losing the slightest details of what happened
to (him)."[100] Thus two worlds of mental awareness became
one: the world of everyday perception and that of hallucination
which may be just as real as the other to the person experiencing it. The unity of these two modes of reality may, however,
appear to be a sign of madness to the onlooker or reader who
experiences only one and cannot comprehend the other.

Nerval's hallucinatory state continued as he followed the
Star and joyously sang a mysterious hymn he believed he had
heard in some other existence.[101] The theme of multiple existences
which will be developed in *Aurélia* is thus introduced. In a
state of ecstasy, he removed his clothes and waited for his soul
to be separated from his body. Unconscious of his earthly surroundings because of his hallucinatory state, he still has an
awareness of his temporal earthly being, and this cognizance
suddenly makes him long for the terrestrial reality and those
he loves. He begs the magnetic Spirit to release him, and he
seems to redescend to earth where he is picked up by soldiers.

The point of view of the work now becomes obvious. There
are three Nervals: the writer attempting lucidly to recount his
experiences; the character about whom he is writing; the inter-
preter or intermediary between the other two and of whom
Nerval the writer is often unaware. The presence of this third
Nerval gives the work its uniqueness and a mysterious quality
that cannot be rationally fathomed. In his narrative Nerval mentions that the mission of a writer is to sincerely analyze what he
experiences in the serious circumstances of life, so he will
continue to describe what he experienced. But the use of expressions such as "I believed" and "I had believed that I saw," while
written by Nerval the writer, poses a question mark to the
authenticity of the experience and seems to belong more to the

third Nerval, the intermediary. It is a matter of doubt whether
Nerval the writer believes the experiences of Nerval the character to be true or illusory, for he uses *Je crus* (I believed) in the
past definite tense which casts doubt in his present state of
mind on their ultimate truth. Yet in this section of the third
chapter of the first part of *Aurélia*, as later elsewhere in the
work, Nerval does seem to be operating on a level of double
awareness: the awareness of one who is experiencing something,
and the awareness of one *watching* another experiencing the
same event. The constant use of the verb "to see," with all its
voyeuristic connotations, forms a superb contrast with its ex-
hibitionistic opposite "to show" or "to make oneself seen." In
Aurélia Nerval gives multiple indications of both voyeurism and
exhibitionism, although they are seldom on a consciously sexual
level. As he says, his soul is "divided between vision and reality."

While the soldiers are with him, Nerval believes he sees the
sky open in such incredible magnificence that he regrets returning to earth:

Immense circles were traced in the infinite, like the orbs that water
forms when something falls into it and disturbs it. Each region,
peopled with radiant figures, was becoming colored, moved and
melted in turn, and a divinity, always the same, smilingly threw
away the furtive masks of its diverse incarnations and, finally im-
perceptible, took refuge in the mystic splendours of the Eastern sky.[102]

Through premonition Nerval thinks he sees two friends appear, but, against his protests, they take away his double, and
when one sees his double Nerval believes that death is near.
Finally the same two friends arrive and "rescue" him.

The double, which appears frequently as a theme in Romantic
literature in the works of Hoffman, Musset, Byron, Poe, and
Baudelaire, is more mystical and premonitional in *Aurélia*, for he
appears just at the onset of madness. The point of view of the
work becomes now even more complex, for Nerval the character
is watching another Nerval, the Double, just as Nerval the
writer is observing Nerval the character. One is tempted to say
that here in rudimentary form is an early example of *composition en abyme*.[103] The Double in *Aurélia* serves as an omen

of death, of guilt, of alienation, and evidences clearly a schizophrenic tendency in Nerval.

At the same time, the following day Nerval succumbed to a
state that lasted several days, a state in which he recognized no
one and lost "the meaning and liaison of images which presented themselves to (him)." He was taken to an asylum.
He writes:

Many relatives and friends visited me without my being aware of it.
For me the only difference between waking and sleeping was that
in the former everything was transfigured. Each person who approached me seemed changed. Material objects appeared in a
penumbra which modified their forms, and plays of light and combinations of colors were distorted in such a way as to keep me in
a constant series of interrelated impressions whose credibility was
continued in the dream state, more abstracted as it was from
exterior elements.[104]

In this world of madness the world of dreams is reality, and
reality itself is transfigured to conform to, and lead into, the
world of dreams. Nerval's descriptions in this section, as in the
recounting elsewhere of his dreams, are reminiscent of later
Surrealist movies in which reality is transformed, and black-and-
white and highly colored objects and images are interwoven,
distorted, and changed in order to produce a superreality. In
Surrealism, however, this is artificially induced; in Nerval's
works it is a natural product of his mental state.

The fourth chapter recounts a dream which has the banks
of the Rhine for locale. Nerval enters a house that seems to
belong to a deceased relative, a painter dead for more than
a century.[105] A servant tells him to lie down, and while on the
bed he notices opposite him a rustic clock with a bird who
begins to talk like a person. Nerval believes that the soul of
his ancestor is in the bird which speaks of living and dead mem-
bers of his family as if they existed simultaneously. But the
writer becomes sleepy and confused and feels himself drawn
into a chasm of the earth. There he sees an old man who had
spoken to him with the voice of the bird. Nerval is given to
understand that "our ancestors take the form of certain animals
in order to visit us on earth, and that thus they are present as

silent observers of the various phases of our existence."[106] The old man accompanies him to a house nearby of which the poet says, "I understand that it had existed in some other time and that in this world that I was visiting the ghosts of material things accompanied those of human bodies."[107] Nerval enters the house, sees people that he has known, and suddenly realizes that everything that has been still exists. The old man tells him, "Oblivion does not exist in the accepted sense, but the earth itself is a material body whose soul is the sum of the souls it contains. Matter can perish no more than mind, but it can be modified according to good and evil. Our past and future are solidary. We live in our race and our race lives in us."[108] Nerval then sees an uninterrupted chain of men and women in whom he was and who were himself, and the impression comes to him that the phenomenon of space is analagous to that of time: A century of action can be concentrated in a minute of dream. The import of this part of the dream is obviously a search in the past for identity with his family and loved ones, and a reassurance that death, which he has feared, is not a state of nothingness, but of eternal life.

In the dream, everything about him was changing. The spirit with whom he was talking did not look the same and was receiving ideas from Nerval rather than communicating them to him. The writer's sense of guilt tells him that he has perhaps probed too far.[109] Then he sees himself wandering in the streets of a populous and unknown city where he is struck by certain individuals who know how to keep their fierce individuality. These are the pre-Adamites who represent the purity of primitive races. There follows a description of pre-Adamite humanity as Nerval goes back through the ages as an archeologist uncovering city upon city. He appears to desire to assuage his guilt, which he feels even in the dream, in a quest for purity that he cannot really know because he is a descendant of Adam, and original sin lies heavy upon him. The sin appears to be sexual, for much of Christianity believes that when Eve and Adam ate the forbidden fruit they suddenly realized they were naked and thus sex rather than disobedience became the cause of sin.

In the dream, the original race was simple in custom, loving and just, clever, strong, and ingenious. It was the peaceful conqueror of the blind masses who had so often invaded its heritage. Its most striking characteristic is that, unlike Adam, it is pure although it has conquered innocence and thus attained a semidivine state. Nerval is so moved by these people that he begins to weep because he knows he cannot stay in this lost paradise for he is guilty, an Adamite.

The narrative then shifts to the present as Nerval tells that he was in a cataleptic state for several days and that this state was scientifically explained to him. But his experiences in the "other" world have resolved for him the problem of the immortality of the soul and the existence of God. He has been given certain signs of the eternal existence of his family and friends who are separated from him only by time. It is evident that the function of the dream is a redeeming one because it is the only worthy response to despair.

Another dream is recounted in the following chapter. Again Nerval finds himself in a room in the house of his ancestor. In it are three women representing relatives and friends of his youth. Their characteristics, as those of the Fates, pass from one to the other as if they had lived the same life and each was composed of all. This is suggestive not only of Nerval's myth of the ideal female, but also of the oniric unity of beings. One of the women speaks to him, and in her arms she is holding a hollyhock which symbolizes a cyclical recurrence. But she disappears, and the poet cries, "Oh, don't flee, for nature dies with you."[110] Then, in a garden, he hurls himself at a fragment of broken wall at the foot of which is the bust of a woman which he is convinced is hers. The garden meanwhile has taken on the aspect of a cemetery, and voices say, "The universe is in darkness."[111] This dream is ominous and is a premonition of the death of Aurélia.

Later he learned that Aurélia had died, but exhibited a peculiar lack of emotion upon hearing the news.[112] He remarks that he was only vaguely unhappy because he felt that he, too, was dying and knew they would meet in another world; that she belonged to him more in death than she had in life. At this point in time his health had been restored, but his mind had not yet returned to normal. He relates his stay at Dr. Blanche's, one incident of which is striking. Nerval executed a series of frescoes to realize his thoughts and painted the Queen of Sheba, an idealized Aurélia as she appeared to him in his dreams. Since these frescoes did actually exist,[113] it is evident that by 1841, at the latest, the concept and myth of the Divine Woman had already formed in the poet's mind.

While at Doctor Blanche's, he also thought much about cabalistic lore, and, in his search for himself, reverts to the past for knowledge and comfort. As if he personally remembers it, he goes back to the first pact made by the genii by means of talismans. He says, "I had tried to reunite the stones of the sacred tablets and to represent the first seven Elohim who had shared the world around them."[114] The number seven had mystical connotations for Nerval, as it does for most mystics. Earlier, in *Aurélia,* he had told his uncle, "We are seven." The uncle replied, "That's the typical number of the human family, and by extension seven times seven and so on."[115] Although Nerval was confused by this statement, it seems possible that the uncle was referring to the seven human types represented by the planets of the ancients. In astrology everyone has two major planets, a birth planet and a rising one. Thus there are seven times seven possible connotations.

In the eighth chapter, Nerval describes the geological history of the earth as well as its supposed spiritual history. He dreamed that he had been transported to a dark planet where the first seeds of creation were struggling. Wild plants and reptiles appeared; monsters gave way to man, wild beasts, fishes, and birds as harmony and beauty began to reign. Nerval asked himself who created this miracle, and then answered:

A radiant goddess guided the rapid evolution of man through these new *metamorphoses.* A distinct race was then established: beginning with birds it also included animals, fish, and reptiles. These were the Divas, Péris, undines and salamanders.[116]

One of the Elohim thought of creating a fifth race composed of elements of the earth called Afrites, who in William Beckford's *Vathek* were guardians of Eblis, the lord of fire. The creation of the Afrites caused a complete revolution among the spirits, and bloody wars took place. The secrets of the ancients were saved by the necromancers in their caves while a new covenant was formed by Noah and God. After describing the great Flood, Nerval sketches a portrait of a woman abandoned by her brothers. Over her head is the star of evening which is reminiscent of the seventeenth Tarot card. This star is the star of hope and the card itself symbolizes the zodiacal sign of Aquarius and the hope of rebirth—the equivalent of the biblical rainbow. Nerval asserts that throughout history repetitions of the carnage took place, and everywhere there was the symbol of the suffering eternal mother (Isis, Cybèle, Virgin Mary). This section is one of the best examples of Nerval's syncretism, for here he mixes in several pages of great stylistic beauty, cabalistic lore, personal beliefs, and biblical myth.

In the ninth and tenth chapters, Nerval moves from the period of his first mental crisis (1841) to a period ten years later in which the second major one occurred. The series of what Nerval calls "strange dreams" recurred during this period, after the hiatus of a decade. In one, preoccupied with a book dealing with religion, he is walking in the country and hears a bird which reminds him of the bird whose form his uncle had taken. He perceives this to be a bad omen. Then he meets a friend who shows him his property; he admires the view, falls, hurts himself, and believes he is dying. (The parallels with the signs of the first descent into madness are striking.) Feverish, he returns home and then remembers that the view was of the cemetery in which Aurélia was buried. He regrets that death had not reunited him with her. But guilt, a feeling deeply experienced in the siege of madness in 1841, reappears and takes the form of regret for the facile loves he has experienced since Aurélia's death.

The guilt is basically sexual, and it raises the problem of Nerval's concept of love and the sexual experience. Like Gide, Nerval seems to dissociate the two. His earlier feeling of guilt about Jenny Colon appears to have been based on a sexual indiscretion which had marred what should have been a transcendent platonic love. This same love, now for Jenny/Aurélia, has been soiled by sexual experiences with women whom he did not love. Caught between the ideal and the mundane, Nerval finds himself in a constant quandary, for to him the two worlds can be no more reconciled than can the mystic world he perceives in his dreams and that of his quotidian existence. Thus it is not surprising to discover that the writer, instead of recounting his dreams, will question them. But Aurélia no longer appears in his dreams, and the first ones of this period are about a fatal race unleashed in the middle of the ideal world that he had formerly seen and of which Aurélia was queen.

The Double also reappears in more frightening form. He is the same spirit who had menaced him in the fifth chapter when he entered the home of the family of the pure in the mysterious city. Now, however, he is no longer dressed in white, but in the garb of an Eastern prince. Nerval rushes toward him, menaces him, but when the spirit turns around the poet sees his own face, his whole being idealized and grown. He does not know how to explain that in his mind terrestrial events could coincide with those of the supernatural world. He seeks the identity of the spirit who is he and yet outside of him. Now he begins to question his dreams, whereas he had only presented them in the first eight chapters. Jean Richer writes:

"The idea of questioning sleep came to me." This systematic recourse to oneiromancy indicates, it seems, a change of attitude with regard to the dream. The series of great dreams related in the first eight chapters is offered as an exhibition. They are, as it were, passively experienced by the dreamer who is the theatre for them. Beginning with the moment when the dream is sought for its value as a symbol, when one claims to draw indications about the conduct to follow in life from it by seeking premonitions in it, the dreamer becomes partly an operator, an experimenter. He intervenes actively; his attitude ceases to be passive. This is perhaps the sort of dividing the awareness in two which then takes place and gives birth to the experience of the *double* related in the rest of the chapter . . .[117]

On this subject Nerval himself writes:

Whatever the case, I believe the human imagination has not invented anything that is not true either in this world or in the others, and I was unable to doubt what I had *seen* so distinctly. I had a terrible idea. Every man has a double . . .[118]

Nerval finds that in all men "there is a spectator and an actor, one who speaks and one who answers. The Orientals saw two enemies in this fact, the good and evil geniuses in man.[119] He wonders if he is the good or the bad, but he knows that the Double is hostile to him and that Aurélia is no longer his.

The presence of the Double necessarily confuses the quest because the Double exists in a mythical past, in an apparent present, as well as in an imagined future. There would appear to be no way of avoiding him, and yet Nerval does not yet seem to know that only through understanding the Other can he understand himself, for the Double could easily be interpreted as part of a schizophrenic personality, other aspects of which have already been noted in earlier sections of the work. Nerval hears of a mystic marriage, which is his own, in which the Double was going to profit from the error of the writer's friends and of Aurélia herself, none of whom sees the Double for what he is. This section of the work, although powerful in its emotional impact, is somewhat confusing. It is easy to understand that Nerval's friends see him as double—the witty, gentle companion and the madman, but why Aurélia is unable to see that it is the Double whom she is going to marry is less clear unless we assume logically (which is not always easy to do with Nerval) that the Double represents the better side of the man. If such is so, then Nerval's despair is more than understandable because once again he feels that he himself is damned in his terrestrial form. Desperate, Nerval decides that he must fight the "fatal spirit" with the arms of tradition and knowledge. "Whatever he does in the shadows and the night, I exist," the author writes, "and to conquer him I have all the time left to me to live on earth."[120] But at the beginning of the tenth chapter Nerval wonders if he can paint the strange despair which these ideas gradually caused him. This last chapter of Part I marks the end of the major downward trend of the book. He has reached the lowest depths of dejection, and the dream itself has refused to fulfill its salutory function. The poet sees himself destined to despair and nothingness.

The same images found in the second chapter reappear in this second bout with madness. Nerval dreams that he is approaching a vast lighted beach, but there is no sun. (The sun never appears in dreams.) He climbs toward a castle on the coast and sees an immense city on the other side, a city similar to that of the dream recounted in the fifth chapter. In terms reminiscent of the Adoniram section of *Voyage en Orient*, he describes an atelier where an enormous animal is being constructed. Here he finds the primitive fire which animated the first beings. But this is the Cainite city, the infernal city of fire in which alchemy is realized. There he recognizes certain people and hears of the marriage of Aurélia and his double. Distraught, he frightens the inhabitants, goes to the throne, and makes a magic sign. He then hears the dolorous cry of a woman, falls to the floor, and, weeping, begins to pray. Yet the voice does not belong to the dream. "...It was the voice of a living person, yet for me it was the voice and accent of Aurélia."[121] Back in the reality of the asylum, he is astonished to find that no one has heard the voice. Guilt is his dominant emotion, for he feels that he has disturbed the harmony of the universe from which his soul drew the certainty of an immortal existence. He writes, "Perhaps I was damned for having offended divine law, for having wished to penetrate a frightful mystery."[122] He is completely damned because he has failed both sexually and spiritually.

Part II begins with the epigraph "Eurydice! Eurydice!" which echoes his poignant plight. As Orpheus had lost his beloved, Nerval has lost Aurélia forever. This cry of despair links the two sections of the book. The first chapter of the second part begins, "Lost a second time!"[123] Nerval is now convinced that he must die without hope. "What then is death? If only it were nothingness! Would to God it were! But God himself cannot make death a nothingness. Why is it that for the first time in so long I think of *Him*?"[124] Nerval is aware that his system has failed:

The fatal system which was created in my mind did not admit that single royalty, or rather it was absorbed in the sum of all beings . . . It was the God of Lucretius, powerless and lost in his own immensity.[125]

The memory that Aurélia believed in God and Jesus upsets him, for he had wept on hearing her pronounce His name.

The form of this section of the work is quite different from what has preceded it: it is basically a dramatic monologue with highly imaged and emotional language. The mood being more intense, the writer's pathos is heightened. But the narration then shifts to Nerval the author writing *Aurélia*, and the mood becomes more rational and philosophical:

When the soul drifts uncertainly between life and the dream, between the disorder of the mind and the return to cool reflection, one must seek help in religious thought. I have never been able to find this help in that philosophy which offers us only egotistical maxims or at most empty experience and bitter doubts. It struggles against moral anguish by annihilating sensibility. Like surgery it can only cut out the organ that makes us suffer. But for us born in the days of revolutions and storms, when all beliefs have been shattered, raised at best in that vague faith that is content with a few external observances, the indifferent adhesion to which is possibly worse than impiety and heresy—it is very difficult for us, when we feel the need, to reconstruct the mystic edifice which the innocent and simple have already built in their hearts. "The tree of knowledge is not the tree of life!" Yet can we cast from our minds all the good and evil that so many intelligent generations poured into them? Ignorance cannot be learned.[126]

Like many of his contemporaries, Nerval was faced with an impossible choice between reason and faith. He is not yet ready to accept faith, although, in the passage quoted above, he does seem to be less despairing than in the lyrical section which preceded it by the very fact that he is even considering faith. His ideal is a spiritual unity of science and Christianity, a syncretic religion, but he is uncertain and frightened of the words he has just written:

These are blasphemies. Christian humility cannot speak that way. Such thoughts are far from making the soul more receptive. They wear on their forehead the brilliant rays of pride of Satan's crown . . . A pact with God Himself? . . . O science! O vanity![127]

Nerval returns from his informal and exclamatory thoughts to straight narration. He recounts that he read some cabalistic books and that he is convinced that the past has great revelations for the present, even though some of the works are incomplete or have been falsified by time or people. He attempted to perceive the correspondences between the real world and the world of spirits:

The earth, its inhabitants and their history were the theatre in which the physical actions which prepared the existence and the situation of the immortal beings attached to its destiny were carried out. Without disturbing the impenetrable mystery of the eternity of worlds, my thoughts went back to the epoch when the sun, like the plant which represents it, which with its bowed head follows its course in the skies, sowed on earth the fecund seeds of plants and animals. It was nothing other than fire itself which, being a composite of souls, instinctively formulated the communal dwelling. The Spirit of the Godhead, reproduced and, so to speak, reflected on the earth, became the common type of human souls, of which, consequently, each one was both man and God. Such were the Elohim.[128]

But the Elohim were of the race of Fire as opposed to the children of Adam, and Nerval's religious confusion remains.

Unhappy, and therefore thinking of the misery of others, Nerval visits a sick friend who, having come close to death, tells him that God is everywhere. Later, thinking of this man, Nerval exclaims, "God is with him.... But He is no longer with me. O misery, I have driven Him from me; I have threatened Him; I have blasphemed."[129] A remarkable psychological phenomenon takes place in this part of *Aurélia*. Nerval's sense of inferiority as well as what appears to be a compensatory sense of superiority is even more pronounced than in earlier sections of the work. The inferiority is usually related to his guilt, be it sexual or religious. The superiority is found in his being mind proud. He feels he can challenge Christianity because of his wealth of mystic lore and knowledge, but this challenge does not answer his questions, and he is thrown into another state of dejection because he preferred the creature to the Creator, has deified his beloved, and adored, according to pagan rites, the woman whose last sigh was consecrated to Christ. Yet he hopes that, if Christian doctrines are true, there is a possibility that God will still pardon him.

But he cannot escape his sense of guilt. Having followed an unknown's funeral procession to the cemetery, he seeks the tomb of Aurélia and is unable to find it. On returning home, he seeks its location on a piece of paper, but, guilty and feeling unworthy, he decides not to return to the cemetery. Instead, he goes to a small town outside Paris where, as a youth, he had spent some happy days. He enters an inn, and the innkeeper tells him of a friend who has killed himself. Nerval retires to his room and dreams. Once again he is in an unknown room, chatting with someone from the outside world (perhaps the friend who committed suicide). He glances in a mirror and seems to think he recognizes a sad and pensive Aurélia who again seems to resemble the figure of Dürer's *Melancholia*. She extends her hand and says, "We shall meet again later . . . at your friend's house."[130] Thinking of her marriage, the curse that separated them, he asks if she has pardoned him. But she has disappeared. Again it is too late. Nerval hears voices saying, "She is lost." Yet she has made a last effort to save him and, guilty, he feels he has missed the supreme moment when pardon was still possible. Hell has claimed him. He awakens and gets on his knees and asks God to forgive him for her sake and hers alone.[131]

Guilt and premonitions of death pervade the third chapter of the second part. Nerval is filled with remorse for a foolishly dissipated life, and his overwhelming guilt is seen in the next dream in which his grandmother reproaches him for loving Aurélia more than his relatives and asks how he can hope for forgiveness. The dream then becomes confused. People from various periods in his life pass before his eyes. Then vaguely-formed plastic images of antiquity appear and seem to resemble symbols whose meaning he grasps only with difficulty. He is attacked for not understanding the secret of life and is again informed that it is too late. Following the pattern in Part I, he wakes, terrified, and is convinced that this is his last day. After a ten-year interval, this idea returns in a more menacing manner. He feels that God had left him these years in order to repent and he had not profited from them. "After the visit of the stone guest, I again sat down to the feast."[132]

In straight narrative Nerval then recounts, as if in defense of himself, his religious background, the influence of an uncle who had interested him in Celtic and Roman antiquities and told him God is the sun, the death of his mother, and the superstitions and strange legends of the countryside in which he was raised. He wants to explain how, off the true road for a long time, he felt brought back to it by the dear memory of a dead person and how the need to believe that she still existed made him rethink his life. "Despair and suicide are the result of certain fatal situations for the one who has no faith in immortality and its pains and joys."[133]

The madness is upon him again: The visions in his sleep reduce him to a state in which he can hardly talk and cannot concentrate or read. His friend George Bell tries to help him overcome his discouragement and Nerval feels he could only have come from Providence, that a Spirit spoke through him. One day, while the two friends were dining together, they heard a woman sing. Her voice reminded Nerval of Aurélia's, and she even resembled her. He wonders if that woman contained Aurélia's spirit.

Despair drives him to make the decision to do no more evil. But since he no longer lies, he is at the mercy of those who do. The illusions begin to return. He sees, for example, a man with a child on his shoulder as St. Christopher with Christ. In Church he hears, "The Virgin Mary is dead and your prayers are useless."[134] Rejected again, he wants to commit suicide. He is also convinced that the end of the world is near because he saw a black sun in an empty sky. He denies the existence of Christ, and soon he is back in a mental hospital. His madness lasted for a month, and then for the next two he wandered about Paris and wrote *Sylvie*. Soon, however, he again became violent and hallucinated. He visited George Bell, fell asleep, and had a new vision. The Goddess appeared and said:

I am the same as Mary, as your mother, the same that you have loved in all forms. At each of your trials I have dropped one of the masks that hide my features, and soon you will see me as I am.[135]

When he awakened he explained to Bell the migration of souls. "It seems to me tonight that I have Napoleon's soul which inspires me and orders me to do great things."[136] So bizarre is his behavior that his friends take him to the Hospice de la Charité. The delirium grows. He is put in a strait jacket, manages to escape from it, and feels equal to a god. Sent to Dr. Emile Blanche at Passy, he sees that up until then everything had been an illusion, but the promises made to him by the goddess Isis seemed to become realized through a series of trials that he, like Tamino in Mozart's *The Magic Flute*, was destined to undergo.

The account in the sixth chapter of Nerval's third major incarceration is one of the most horrifying accounts of madness in all literature. His fellow inmates seem to influence the stars, and one who walked in circles seemed to control the course of the sun; another regulated the course of the hours. Celestial spirits had taken human forms. In this cosmos Nerval's role was to reestablish universal harmony by means of cabalistic art and seek a solution by evoking the occult forces of various religions. He was bathed by the Valkyries who were raising him to immortality by cleansing his body of its impurities. There seemed to be a vast conspiracy of all animate beings to reestablish the world's harmony, and communication took place by means of the magnetism of the stars. The moon was the refuge of fraternal souls who, freed of their mortal frames, worked more freely for the regeneration of the universe. The horror of the dream, despite the beauty of its presentation and its vision of brotherhood and harmony, lies in the fact that it is less related, if at all attached to, earthly reality than any of those previously described. In this hallucination, for it is more a hallucination than a dream, Nerval has left this world completely behind and become one with the forces beyond man's comprehension. Even when he "awakes" from the dream, he does not return to quotidian reality. He relates that he wandered in shadows for two hours, and then, as the sun rose, he prayed to it and his real life began. But this real life is still in the world of hallucination, for he is assured that he is undergoing the tests of the sacred initiation, that he is the hero watched over by the gods. Suddenly everything in nature takes on new aspects. Nerval hears secret voices from plants, trees, animals, and insects which encourage and warn him. He becomes aware of harmonies hitherto unknown and wonders:

How have I been able to live so long outside Nature without identifying with it? Everything lives, acts, corresponds; the magnetic rays that emanate from myself or from others traverse the infinite chain of created things without obstacle. It is a transparent network which covers the world, and its slender threads communicate themselves by degrees to the planets and stars. A captive now on earth, I commune with the astral choir which shares in my joys and sorrows.[137]

This passage, like those that immediately follow it, is of crucial importance for an understanding of Nerval. Unlike his contemporaries, who believed in the theory of correspondences, Nerval not only perceives these correspondences, but experiences them on a mystic, rather than a rational or drug-induced, level. In his hallucinations they become part of a superreality, a reality that can be achieved only in what those who have not experienced them would call states of madness. Nerval becomes part of the cosmos, but he makes no attempt, as does Baudelaire in his sonnet "Corréspondances," to indicate the way for others to achieve awareness of the original harmony. Nerval is not only aware of this harmony but momentarily participates in it as an actor rather than a philosopher or teacher-poet. In this passage of identification and participation, Nerval, although in a hallucinatory state, achieves for the first time in *Aurélia* a harmony, a sense of place and self that has been heretofore denied him, and, although there are still pitfalls, he comes closer to his goal in his quest for himself. Much as Tamino in Mozart's *The Magic Flute*, he is undergoing an initiation into the mysteries of self and the universe.

But there are still obstacles to be surmounted and questions to be answered. The major one is the problem of evil:

". . . It has been rightly said nothing is indifferent, nothing powerless in the universe. An atom can dissolve everything or save everything.

"What terror! *There* is the universal distinction between good and evil. Is my soul the indestructible molecule, the sphere that can be inflated by a little air, which finds its place in nature, or is it that very void, which is the image of the nothingness that disappears in the immensity? Or could it be that fatal particle destined to undergo in all its transformations the vengeance of powerful beings?" Thus I was led to take account of my life and even of my previous existences. By proving to myself that I was good I proved to myself that I had

always been so. "And if I have been evil," I said to myself, "will not
my present life be a sufficient expiation?" The thought reassured me
but did not remove some of the fear of being forever classified with
the unhappy.[138]

Thoughts of Isis and the Virgin Mary return, and Nerval wonders, "What can she, conquered and perhaps oppressed, do
for her poor children?"[139]

At this point the narrative abruptly changes to what must
be called an interlude in which Nerval describes his room
in the asylum. Following this section there is a lacuna in the
text in which certain editors have inserted letters that Nerval
wrote to Jenny Colon, but since they are not in the original
manuscript they will not be discussed because Nerval's critics
do not know exactly which letters they are.[140]

The story is continued with the recounting of another hallucination in which, in a sort of Oriental pavilion, Nerval saw
a painting of an enormous woman with various parts of her cut
off as if by a sword. On the other walls women of other races
and all social classes were painted in similar fashion:

It was the history of all crime . . . "There," I said to myself, "is what
the power bestowed on man has produced. He has little by little
destroyed and cut into a thousand pieces the eternal type of beauty
so that the races are more and more losing their strength and perfection . . ."[141]

He is interrupted in his contemplation by the arrival of his
doctor who, trying to get Nerval out of his somber mood, shows
him a man "who could neither see nor speak," and who, refusing
to eat, has been fed through a tube in his stomach. Seeing
someone suffering more than he, Nerval suddenly takes an
interest in this man whom he sees as a brother or a double.
Because of his sympathy, kindness, and will power, Nerval helps
the young man, whom he calls Saturninus, to become better,
and, in so doing, improves his own psychic state.

The female divinity, in Indian dress, then appears to him.
Smiling, she says:

The trial which you have undergone is coming to an end. Those
countless stairways that tired you so in coming down and going up

were the very bonds of old illusions that confused your thoughts. Now remember the day you implored the Holy Virgin and, thinking her dead, went mad. Your vow had to be carried to her by a simple soul, one free of earthly ties. She appeared near to you, and that is why I have been permitted to come to encourage you.[142]

Nerval is nearing the end of his quest. He has been saved, at least temporarily, from his madness and his doubts. His personality, through his identification with, and compassion for, his brother or double Saturninus, has been reintegrated, and yet he has returned from a marvelous, if often horrifying, voyage to worlds few men ever see and of which most are unaware.

The final section of *Aurélia* is called "Mémorables" ("Memorabilia"), and it contains the impressions of certain dreams which followed the one of the goddess in Indian costume. In this part Nerval not only sees the woman he loved radiant and transfigured, but reads the word "pardon" written in Christ's blood. Nerval's syncretism is again evident in these dreams. The other gods and goddesses have also been pardoned by Christ, but they still exist. The dreams end in a hope for peace:

I encouraged myself in an audacious undertaking. I resolved to fix the dream state and learn its secret. "Why not," I said to myself, "at last force those mystic gates, armed with all my will power, and dominate my sensations instead of being subject to them? Is it not possible to subdue this fascinating, dread chimera, to impose an order on these spirits of the night which play with our reason? Sleep occupies a third of our life. It is the consolation for the sorrows of our days or the pain of their pleasures. But I have never experienced rest in sleep. After a few minutes of sluggishness a new life begins, freed from the condition of time and place and doubtless similar to that state which awaits us after death. Who knows if a link does not exist between these two existences and if it is not possible for the soul to unite them now![143]

The insights of Nerval are direct predecessors of the theories of Freud, and his discussions of dreams and their importance are a landmark in French literature. Nerval relates that he devoted himself to the discovery of the meaning of his dreams:

I believed I understood that there existed a bond between the external and internal worlds, that only our inattention or mental disorders falsified the apparent relationships between them, and this explained the strangeness of certain pictures which are similar to those grimacing reflections of real objects which move on the surface of troubled waters.[144]

The final paragraph of *Aurélia* recapitulates many of the themes found in the work and proves that this is a finished piece of literature:

The treatment I had received had already brought me back to the affection of family and friends, and I could judge more sanely the world of illusions in which I lived for some time. Just the same I feel happy with the convictions I had acquired and I compare that series of trials that I experienced to that which for the ancients represented the idea of a descent into hell.[145]

Knowledge has come to Nerval through his experiences. His quest for himself has been completed; his guilt has been assuaged; he has been forgiven for his unstated sins through the intercession of Aurélia. Yet the work ends on a tentative note, for just as he had been cured before and now once again is well, there is always the implicit danger of a relapse into a hell far worse than the ones he had previously experienced. As far back as 1840, in his preface to *Faust* and the *Second Faust*, he had written:

Indeed, Helen, drawn from her shadowy dwelling in Hades by the desire of Faust, is seen once again surrounded by her women before the peristyle of her palace in Argos at the very moment in which she has just embarked on her native shores, brought back by Menelaus from Egypt to which she had fled after the fall of Troy. Is the memory which recreates itself present here? Or do the same things that have happened reproduce themselves a second time in the same details? This is one of those frightening hallucinations of the dream and even of certain instants of life where it seems that one redoes an already performed action and says again words already spoken, foreseeing successively the things that are going to happen.[146]

The past, thus, can repeat itself in a frightening manner.

In many ways *Aurélia* is in the lineage of Goethe's *Faust*.

From an early age Nerval had been haunted by the hero of the German poet, and the parallels between Nerval's odyssey and that of Faust are striking. One is tempted to say that, influenced by Faust, Nerval subconsciously takes on many of his characteristics in *Aurélia*. In 1828 he wrote the following in his preface to the first edition of *Faust*:

Faust possesses this love for science and immortality to the highest degree. It often raises him to the level of a god or the idea we form of a god, and yet all in him is natural and supposable, for if he has all the grandeur and strength of humanity he also has all its weaknesses. By asking hell for the help heaven has refused him, his first thought was doubtless the happiness of his fellow men and universal knowledge. He hoped by means of knowledge to obtain the absolution of his audacity from God. But the love of a young girl sufficed to upset all his chimeras. It is the apple of Eden which, instead of knowledge and life, offers the enjoyment of a moment and an eternity of tortures.[147]

In many ways this could stand as a summary of *Aurélia*. As Jenny Colon was for Nerval, so Helen was for Faust. Both cross time with the rapidity of a dream and both represent an eternal type. Nerval remarks that Faust's search for Helen was almost the descent into Hades of Orpheus. Helen has replaced Gretchen (Marguerite) as Aurélia has replaced Jenny Colon. "There is therefore a love of intelligence, of dream and madness which succeeds the completely naive and very human love of Marguerite in his heart."[148]

Aurélia is a unique work in which Nerval, through the revelation of his crises, makes the reader reevaluate the distinction between sanity and madness, between reality and the dream. His portrayal of a world unknown to most men is often hallucinatory, yet it is expressed in very clear terms. The images are colorful and evocative, the philosophy clearly defined. If his study of the dream has strong Freudian overtones, his awareness of the collective memories of the race is distinctly Jungian. He reexperiences the history of the human race through his hallucinations and dreams, and in *Aurélia* we witness the progress of the subconscious to the level of the conscious. He takes part in a world of cosmogonies and religions that are often in apparent contradiction, and relates his personal experiences as memories of the past, of previous existences of which he alone is aware. But all becomes an eternal present because the past is always part of us and will determine the future as well as the present. To the seer, and Nerval certainly has the tone of one, everything that has existed still exists. Life is a quest for knowledge both of self and of the cosmos, but the knowledge is always within the seeker waiting to be revealed.

Aurélia is one of the most unique works of its period. Its influence has, however, been great. Echoes of it are to be found in the works of Rimbaud, Proust, and the Surrealists as well as in the works of the psychoanalytic school. It is not the first, but one of the most important documents concerning one man's search for himself and therefore for salvation.

CHAPTER 4

The Journalist-Critic

F OR more than twenty years Nerval contributed articles, essays, and occasional pieces to the leading publications of his epoch. That his contributions were highly regarded is attested to by his friend Théophile Gautier.[1] Although it may be difficult to determine the boundary between criticism and journalism, it may be said with assurance that Nerval was an important critic of his era, of its mores, literature, music, and aberrations. Often this criticism is written in journalistic style: it gives the impression of being written for a deadline and lacks the depth and polish of his other prose writings. In many of his essays, however, such as those on Heine, the future of tragedy, Voltaire's theatre, Greek drama, Donizetti's *La Favorite,* his prefaces to *Faust,* his essays on German poetry and the French poets of the sixteenth century, the prose is as fine and carefully written as that of the best criticism of his contemporaries.

Undoubtedly the writer of his period who was the best read and had the vastest scope in his readings, Nerval was knowledgeable in ancient literatures, all modern European literatures of importance, Eastern literature, and the works of the mystic writers of all periods and places. This knowledge is staggering in both its breadth and depth. His comments on music, and especially opera, are, if not the most profound, exceedingly penetrating for one who was not a professional musician. Most of his judgments on literature and music, although they were not often those of his contemporaries, seem quite modern. His appreciation of Berlioz and Wagner, of certain of Donizetti's bel canto operas, his judgments of Corneille, Voltaire, Balzac, Hugo, and Marivaux are those held by most twentieth-century critics.

147

Having an essentially creative mind, Nerval thought of criticism as a secondary art, for literature had to precede it. He believed that criticism owed its origin and strength to literary and artistic decadence and always followed an epoch of great works which it tries to explain to the masses. Thus, Nerval claims, it offends good human sense. Yet he finds criticism necessary in his era because four groups stifled the free expression of the artistic mind. He often attacks the bourgeois public for its abysmal taste, and just as often the critics who pander to that taste. He writes, "... everything seems written by porters,—for porters!"[2] Not only are the public and the critics to be blamed for the low quality of art being produced, but the Church, University, and managers of theatres and opera houses as well. Both the Church and the University discourage innovations and scorn works that do not conform to fixed forms and rules. If the critics encourage the public's taste for melodrama and vaudeville, the Church and University praise dead forms that have little contemporary meaning. The doors of many of the great theatres are closed to innovative artists by administrations fearful of financial loss, and thus these theatres are artistically unadventurous. In writing of the revival of Spontini's *Fernand Cortez* in 1840, Nerval says, "If Gluck or Mozart were to return today in person they would be treated as first place winners of the Prix de Rome. They (the administration of the Opéra) love great men, but they love them dead."[3]

In his essays, Nerval shows himself most often to be modern without being exclusively Romantic. He does not praise the new just because of its novelty, nor does he accept the old because of its venerability. He has certain standards that must be met, and he judges the work of art according to whether the writer or composer has achieved these standards. Nerval judges works of the past not only for their intrinsic worth, but for their relevance to his own society. He recognizes Corneille's greatness as a playwright, but finds that the ideas on which his plays are based are dated. Only in times of revolution or war do his plays achieve success. (This has been amply illustrated by the fortune of Corneille's plays since Nerval's own time.) Racine is the more universal playwright because love is a subject always of interest and of the moment. In judging modern works,

Nerval's standard of criticism is basically whether the work is natural, that is to say, whether it conforms to reality. It is for this reason that he prefers Hugo to Scribe, or the actor Bocage to Talma. Yet this standard of naturalness may be modified if the creator has achieved his intention. In his essay on Mademoiselle Mars, Nerval writes:

A work of art is like a growing plant by virtue of its inherent characteristics. You would perhaps have hoped that the oak was a little less strong and the grass a bit less weak. Don't be angry at the oak or grass for that; they cannot become more and have done nothing to become what they are. There they are as their seed requires them to be.

So it is with works of art . . . Every time one has done what one wanted to do one has done well.[4]

The critic thus judges also by the artist's intention and whether he has fulfilled it.

For Nerval, the work of art needs an absolute and precise form, for without it all is trouble and confusion. Thus his natural tendencies lead him to appreciate classic art in a manner many of his contemporaries did not. His sense of aesthetic balance, unequalled in his time, permits him to take a reasonable approach in his judgments on the Classic-Romantic controversy. He likes the works of both Hugo and Racine and feels it is ridiculous to compare them. Unlike his eighteenth-century predecessors, Nerval believes in transformations rather than progress in the arts. There is little that is new in subject matter, just different ways of treating it. Thus he finds Hamlet to be an Elizabethan Orestes and Romeo and Juliet an English Pyramus and Thisbe. Yet artists should look to the future for "the present is only a word, and the past belongs only to the dead."[5] This, however, is not a dismissal of the great works of the past, but merely an admonition to avoid literal translations of them into the present.

In almost Tainian terms, Nerval sees literature as an expression of its time, the result of certain racial, geographical, and temporal factors that have determined it. Thus he finds in the poetry of the French Middle Ages the seeds of all that is to come later in French literature. Plays of different epochs should be played in the style of their epoch as well as in its settings and costumes. If the work of art of a past period has contemporary validity, it will come from the subject and depiction of characters, but to be truly appreciated it must be done in the style of its own period. Racine in frock coats remains Racine, but the work is aesthetically ridiculous. If literature is an expression of its time, then Petrus Borel is a good representative of his generation. Nerval finds that the satanic, frenetic, and bloody aspects of Borel's work reflect his epoch, and therefore his subject matter is not only defensible but valid.

The constituent principle of modern art for Nerval is the representation of the real, the natural, and the form of the work of art should fit the subject. He remarks, "As it has been quite well said the truth is not this or that defined form; the truth is what it can become."[6] Bocage is a great actor because he is himself; he remains a man, not a God. Talent resembles God: it is because it is. For this reason the boulevard actor (Bocage, for example) is better than those at the Comédie-Française because he does not idealize, because the ideal has no real model here on earth. Even the poet must be natural. Nerval writes, "The poet no longer reasons; he executes. He no longer shows his logic but his heart . . . he is himself."[7]

Nerval's ideas are basically impressionistic, personal rather than objective, although objectivity is not often lacking. In general his essays begin with his own ideas on the subject at hand and a discussion of its historical or social context. Then Nerval treats the work under consideration. In his better essays he writes thoroughly perceptive and professional criticism, yet often he recounts in journalistic fashion the plot of the work and concludes with a statement or two about his reaction to it. It is difficult for Nerval, as for any critic, to be completely objective about all works of art, and, perhaps more than most, he lets himself be guided by his emotions and personal interests. Certain subjects—dreams, madness, the bizarre, sexual and platonic love, mysticism—strike sympathetic chords in him, and the work of certain friends such as Dumas or the singing of his idol Jenny Colon are examined less than objectively. Often, as in the case of Dumas, Nerval collaborated with him on certain dramatic pieces to which only Dumas's name was attached. Nerval wryly writes of these in glowing terms, often pointing out the beauty of certain verses he himself had written. Objectivity is more apparent when the work under consideration is historical in origin.

The major concern of his essays is the theatre and the opera and their problems and performances between 1830 and 1851. Few novels and little poetry (except for German poets and the poetry of the Renaissance) come under his scrutiny. Nerval's interest in the theatre was great, and throughout his life he wrote or projected the writing of many plays. His desire, both financially and aesthetically, was to become a successful playwright. His interest in opera is attached to his love for the theatre and was certainly nurtured by his infatuation with the singer Jenny Colon, but this interest lasted long after her death. Nerval had a superb knowledge of world theatre, and his most important criticism is found mainly in essays on that field.

In general, Nerval is unhappy with the state of French drama in the Romantic period. With the exception of Dumas and Hugo (whose *Ruy Blas* he sees as the poet's most original and successful work) and Musset, Nerval finds little of true value in the theatre of his epoch, be it in the classical imitations, vaudeville or dull comedies praised by the critics, except in the truly great plays of the past that were being revived.

One of the problems Nerval continually faced in his criticism was the distinction between *le drame* and tragedy. Although he finds it difficult to distinguish between drama and tragedy, he several times uses analogies between painting (Hamlet) and sculpture (Orestes). He writes, "Would to God that tragedy were still possible! Tragedy is to drama what statuary is to painting. The greatest possible error would be to mix the methods of the two, to add color to one and relief to the other."[8] He wonders whether the distinction between the true and the suitable, the real and the ideal, the possible and the conceivable will be established. In an attempt to distinguish between the two forms of theatre, he says:

Although drama admits particularly the image of chance on the diverse results of human will, brusque contrasts, irregular movements, the diversely colored aspects of common and independent life; although tragedy is more willingly concerned with fatal or providential facts, with chosen forms and actions, with harmonious and regular movements, with economical and blending nuances and effects besides a more symmetrical design, no one of these two genres can lack more than the other in harmony and real unity, and a perfect idea of this exterior difference and this intimate rapport has been given by comparing tragedy to the works of Greek architecture and drama to the marvels of Gothic art.[9]

Both are valid forms. Why declare one greater than the other except in the individual execution?

It seems to me that the difference between tragedy and drama exists principally in the fatal or providential idea and in the idea of chance and liberty applied systematically to human actions. Fatality dominates ancient history; liberty and chance reign in modern traditions and characters. Paganism shows us its heroes governed by family traditions or divine influences. Christianity shows its heroes free in action and thwarted only by things. Now as one feels behind each ancient character a good or evil, helpful or avenging God who holds the thread of his life, the means which tie and untie the action are always noble and imposing.[10]

Drama, unlike tragedy, since the former obeys the law of chance, often deals with petty details, and heroic and vulgar characters are, of necessity, mixed in an action that is common to both of them. For Nerval this explains the different poetics expressed by Hugo in his *Preface* to *Cromwell*.

Is it to be said now that there is less *convention* and *choice* in the theatrical system of drama than in tragedy? We do not think so. We see only the poet operating according to two different systems. Is Shakespeare *truer* than Aeschylus? Is Rubens *truer* than Raphael? ... One sought the beautiful in a primitive, harmonious, and serious nature, the other in a degraded, exuberant nature that is full of contrasts; but their works have to the same degree the stamp of the grandiose and the ideal, and that is what places them above all the others.[11]

Nerval's attitude toward various forms of theatre is basically unprejudiced. He states that a school is being founded in which the artists seek only the free imitation of nature—subject only to the conditions of interest and lyricism that the great foreign poets had realized. Nerval is optimistic about the future of French drama, for, unlike the theatre of other European countries, it is not overshadowed by former golden ages: that of Shakespeare in England, of Goethe and Schiller in Germany, of Calderón in Spain. Quality rather than genre is what is important to Nerval. In long essays he discusses in detail *le drame merveilleux* in England, Spain, and Germany, and sees a place for it in contemporary French theatre. The Romanesque genre glorified by Shakespeare and Calderón is found again in Dumas's *L'Alchimiste*. He finds the bourgeois drama not necessarily inferior to comedy and tragedy, especially when it follows the concepts, if not the practice, of Diderot whom he admires.

Comedy is the genre in which Nerval finds little of merit in his epoch. In one essay he claims that a good comedy has not been written in twenty years. He praises Marivaux and Rotrou, relates them to their times, gives a sociological background of their theatre, and claims they cannot be imitated. He does see that his contemporary Musset is capable of Romanesque comedy, but little of Musset was produced in his lifetime, so Nerval mentions him just in passing. Nerval prefers eighteenth-century comedy to that of the nineteenth century and finds that the difference between them lies in the fact that the earlier comedy had no humanitarian or social pretention. It corrected no one and neither did it spoil anyone: it was pure literary study.

As to comedy of character, Nerval is not fond of the genre. Its fault is that, in wanting to give too general lessons, it becomes full of contradictions. Nerval writes that he feels that it is a false genre due to Latin decadence. He sees that there is nothing like it in Aristophanes, Shakespeare, or Calderón, considered as comic authors. Although Molière himself gave in on several matters to the classic ideas of his times, Nerval wonders if Alceste is really *the* misanthrope any more than Timon of

Athens is *the* spendthrift, Richard III *the* ambitious one, or Falstaff *the* drunkard.

Nerval is especially perceptive in his treatment of the ancient Greek theatre. He sees it as intrinsically finer than the Classical French theatre because its tragedy causes a more visceral reaction. In it there are no languorous Achilles or gallant Hippolytuses. Its subjects and characters have great interest for all men. In discussing the *Phaedra* of Euripides, he finds asceticism (in the character of Hippolytus with whom he seems to identify) fighting pagan ideas—the unity of the cult against polytheism. Nerval's syncretic interests are found in this essay when he speaks of Hippolytus as the dying martyr consoled by the saint in whom he has faith. Diana is described as the holy virgin, and the subject of the play is the conflict between noble platonic love and eros, a subject that had great personal meaning to Nerval. Another Greek play of which he is fond is the *Prometheus* of Aeschylus which he terms the most grandiose and poetic play of the ancient theatre. He writes:

The poet who dared right in Greece and in full paganism to deny the eternity of Jupiter and announce the coming of a new revealer is certainly the father of that whole family of skeptical poets to whom we owe today *Hamlet, Faust,* and *Manfred*.[12]

It must be noticed that Nerval is most sympathetic to works which relate to his own preoccupations. Playwrights who deal with the dream such as Shakespeare and Calderón, with syncretism such as the Greeks and Goethe, or characters who are prey to or feign madness such as Hamlet and Orestes strike responsive notes in the critic.

Aside from Hugo and Dumas, Nerval spends more time on the works of Scribe than on those of any other contemporary. For him Scribe is above the level of a hack ("...the taste of our century isn't even up to the level of M. Scribe."[13]), and his works have definite dramatic virtues. But Scribe is an incomplete dramatist because he lacks style and basic form. His works, claims Nerval, need the help of music, and therefore he should leave pure literature alone.

Nothing resembles more a complete and significant drama than an opera of Scribe *finished* by Meyerbeer; nothing imitates more the effect not yet realized in French Romanesque comedy, as Shakespeare and Calderón had understood it, than an opéra-comique by Scribe *finished* by Auber.[14]

One would scarcely quarrel with Nerval's assessment of his prolific contemporary.

Nerval's concept of the theatre is in some ways original, although many of his ideas are to be found in Hugo's *Preface to Cromwell.* Foreshadowing Wagner, whose music he heard in Germany in 1854, Nerval is concerned with the unity of the arts. He is much concerned with the structure of a play, with its elements of spectacle, sets, and costumes, with the relationship between words and music to produce great music drama. Although not one of history's great theatrical reformers, he still has many ideas that are in advance of his time and foreshadow those of Wagner and Stanislavsky. But above all, he believes the theatre to be an image of life. In an essay, *Emile or the Smuggler's Dog,* he somewhat humorously states that dogs have as much right to appear in the theatre as man. After all they, too, form part of this world.

Aside from popularizing Goethe and the German poets in France and making very perceptive remarks about their works in his prefaces to his translations of them, Nerval wrote several superb essays on Heine and on the French poets of the sixteenth century. In the former he depicts Heine as a picturesque and sentimental Voltaire and finds the originality of his work to lie in the mixture of the sentimental and skeptical. Quite justly he sees Heine as a man of opposites for whom words do not designate objects. They rather evoke them (as they do in Nerval's own poetry). The critic finds the German poet to be the poet of the senses whose style is basically Greek, and he dubs him a philosophical Aristophanes. Although he does not analyze much of Heine's poetry in detail, his comments on his work as a whole show the overall view and incisiveness of an excellent critic.

A more important work, perhaps, is Nerval's long essay on the French poets of the sixteenth century. In it he proclaims the idea that all primitive literature is national and created for a need. It contains the seeds of all that is to come in the literature of the country. Almost single-handedly Nerval helped revive interest in the literature of the Renaissance and Middle Ages, a literature that had fallen into disrepute in the seventeenth century and had yet to be valued for what it was. True, there was much interest in the Gothic in the second half of the eighteenth century, and Chateaubriand and Walter Scott helped popularize certain aspects of the Middle Ages, but it was Nerval who first wrote at length about the literature of the period. He finds great poetry in the courtly poems, the allegorical poems, and fine literature in the mystery and morality plays, the farces and fabliaux. But he sees this great poetry already in decadence in the sixteenth century except for the works of Villon (written a bit earlier) and Marot. He examines literally the *Défence et illustration de la langue française* of Du Bellay, and takes the author to task for his scorn of the literature that preceded that of his own time. But Nerval sees that one thing that the school of Ronsard created (and influenced the nineteenth-century poet by) was its gracious and light poetry. What offends Nerval, who disliked literary censorship that demanded all-inclusive doctrines and literary hegemony, is that the Pléiade introduced a type of despotism and repulsed the popular in art. For Nerval all was valid if well executed, and doctrinaires, whether of his own century or any other, did not appeal to him. Yet in the poetry of the Renaissance Nerval finds a freshness that had since been lost.

As a music critic Nerval had not only good taste, but many excellent insights. In many ways he was far ahead of his contemporaries in appreciating composers whose music was in advance of their times. Berlioz, unappreciated by his peers and today still more performed abroad than in France where a complete presentation of his masterpiece *Les Troyens* is still to be performed, was respected by Nerval because of the theatrical aspects of his music. Berlioz had, of course, used a number of Nerval's translations of songs from *Faust* for his own *La Damnation de Faust* (his wit and that of Nerval were similar), and Nerval, commenting on a performance of Berlioz's *Mass*, claims, quite rightly, that it belongs as much to the theatre as to the Church. He claims that only Berlioz could have carried off this feat.

The operas that had created furors in Paris in the eighteen thirties, give or take a year—Meyerbeer's *Robert le diable* and *Les Huguenots* and Auber's *La Muette de Portici*—are appreciated by Nerval for their spectacular dramatic effects as well as for the music that underlines these exhibitions of showmanship. Although in our own day the weaknesses of these operas as well as their strengths seem more apparent now that their shock effect has disappeared, it is not surprising that Nerval should have liked them for even Wagner found many significant passages in Meyerbeer.

But Nerval is at his most acute when dealing with operas not already acclaimed before he began to write. For him the libretto was of utmost importance, perhaps because he wrote several libretti. In review after review he speaks of the stupidity of libretti that even good music cannot save. After reading the stories of these forgotten operas by Batton, Onslow, and others, one is amazed that they were ever produced. He remarks that the operatic subjects of his time that were in fashion were those dealing with political and social questions. Yet he feels that the political hero, despite his claim to our intelligence, must be humanized in order to move us. Again, in opera as in theatre, the natural is all-important; abstractions eventually become tiring.

Two operas of which he saw the greatness were Donizetti's *Lucia di Lammermoor* and *La Favorite*. In his essay on *La Favorite* in 1846, Nerval wrote that the singer was no longer a nightingale, but rather a lyric tragedian who must emote and act, a theory similar to Wagner's ideas as well as to Gluck's. Nerval seeks in opera the unity of action and interest that was the principle of old French opera before Italian opera took over. Yet Italy, not France, was reverting to the earlier form and giving an example of the reaction to pure but mere vocal fireworks. This marks, according to Nerval, the end of the rococo, for the new composers were seeking an alliance of poetry, drama, and music. In a letter written to Dr. Emile Blanche from Leipzig on June 30, 1854, he says, speaking of Wagner, "I feel quite disposed in favor of the music, and my theories, that I don't often expose, are rather close to those of Richard Wagner."[15] This was written seven years before the essays on Wagner by Baudelaire and Gautier.

Nerval's training in music is somewhat of a question mark. As a child he studied the piano, but there is little concrete evidence that his studies went further. Yet when he speaks of certain singers, such as Duprez (the first tenor to sing a chest-produced high C) and his beloved Jenny Colon, he appears to know more about the singer's art than the facts warrant. He was at worst a good amateur, but perhaps, as with his knowledge of English, his musical knowledge has been underestimated by the critics.

Nerval's criticism is an important manifestation of his genius. That he was not a critic of the calibre of Sainte-Beuve or Baudelaire is unimportant. He *was* an important critic, and in his essays there is an originality and a lack of personal animosity that mars much of Sainte-Beuve's criticism. His technique, because it is essentially relativistic, is reminiscent of Madame de Staël's. His method is often that of comparison. When he writes of Bocage, he compares him with Talma, of Heine with Voltaire and Aristophanes. He uses the range of Western literature and art as well for comparisons.[16] In writing of the performance of the Bayadères, he compares the dance group to the Bible, ancient art, and the strange life of the clans in Scott's Scotland. Comparisons have the value of relating novelty to known entities, and by making them, Nerval conveys much to his readers.

Nerval generally chooses to write about subjects that interest or haunt him. In 1839 he wrote an essay on an unproduced play *Le Mort vivant* of M. de Chavagneux. The novelty of the story is the hero who is a dead man. The plot revolves around the question of suicide, for Fernand has committed the only crime God does not pardon—suicide, which is worse than murder or impiety. In light of Nerval's predilection with suicide and his eventual taking of his own life, his comments on this work are most telling. So, too, is he fascinated by Shakespeare and Calderón because of their interest in the dream, and in Orestes and Hamlet because of their madness. Oddities intrigue him as well, and he writes stylishly about Catlin's touring Ojibaways and the visits of theatres of the East.

The style of his essays is normally one of repose, but he knows how to use invective, indignation, and satire, as seen in his essay on the Académie Française. Nor is humor alien to his style, although the humor is usually tinged with irony. At their best, his essays are reminiscent of those of Giraudoux in form, style, and subject matter. Giraudoux, like Nerval, was a Germanophile, was greatly interested in the theatre, had an imposing erudition, and besides, paid Nerval the compliment of writing a most perceptive and appreciative essay about him.

Nerval's criticism is as much a part of him as his poetry or works in prose and, like them, reflects his mental attitudes. After 1843 (two years after his first major attack of madness) one notes an increased use of mythological terms and words such as *ombre, sommeil, fantômes* (shadow, sleep, ghosts) just as one finds their increased use in his noncritical writings. The criticism could not help but reflect the man, and, besides its intrinsic worth, it helps us to understand the workings of the mind of a genius whose essence is quite difficult to grasp at any time of his life.

CHAPTER 5

Conclusion

THE twentieth century has justifiably placed Nerval among the great Romantic writers, and for many critics and creative artists of our time he stands above some of his formerly important contemporaries in achievement and in the creation of a new and very modern sensibility in literature. The direct influence of his works is often difficult to gauge, but many of his ideas and techniques are echoed in the writings of the twentieth century. Certain of these ideas, and especially the relationship of the dream to everyday life as well as to the subconscious, were forerunners of theories of Freud and the later practitioners of psychoanalysis. *Aurélia* presages the Surrealist movement and compares more than favorably with works such as Breton's *Nadja* with which it has many similarities. The depiction of the world of hallucination and syncretic beliefs is found again in the works of Rimbaud and in contemporary poets as dissimilar as Henri Michaux and Antoine Artaud. Nerval's concepts of privileged moments, of the coexistence of different time spans, and the involuntary memory are direct predecessors of the works of Proust who, of all French authors, seems the closest to Nerval in sensibility. His view of Nature as a work of art and the world as a theatre in which man plays out his fantasies and obsessions which are predetermined by a capricious destiny is reminiscent of the universe of Giraudoux. Many of Nerval's greatest works are a refracted history of his physical and mental life and his quest for self and meaning in a world that is alien religiously, socially, and intellectually, and they prefigure many of the themes and nightmarish aspects of the writings of Kafka, Adamov, Beckett, and Ionesco.

Nerval was, perhaps unconsciously, an experimenter and revolutionary despite his moderate and balanced critical views about literature in general. Where Lamartine, Vigny, Hugo,

160

and Musset were still writing within a system of prosody that had clarity of expression and direct communication as its object, Nerval, undoubtedly unknown to himself, was writing outside it. Poetic prosody is revolutionized in the *Chimères*, and even Baudelaire, who was perhaps a more consistent and greater genius, did not use the sonnet form or the Alexandrine in the original way Nerval did. Content and a new type of sensitivity are what distinguish Baudelaire's poetry, but his use of poetic forms is not revolutionary. He uses the Alexandrine with the modifications created by his predecessors in the Romantic movement, but there is nothing essentially new in his use of it. Nerval, with his bizarre but meaningful use of punctuation to express a world of doubt, questions, silences, and exclamations, with his choice of exotic and evocative proper names, brings new rhythms into French poetry, rhythms which reverberate long after the poems are read. His prose at its best is marked by its lyrical use of language to express worlds of memory, dreams, and hallucinations. He was not a storyteller in the accepted sense of the term because his prose works tend to be romanticized, anguished, and often hallucinatory personal reminiscences. His art and life are indivisible, but he was able through his conscious artistry to give form to the former. Above all, Nerval was an artist who attempted in literature to probe the very essence of his own being and, in so doing, created a great fictional character of himself. His quest for the personal peace that comes from knowledge of oneself, although unsuccessful in his life, is attained in his art where he achieves knowledge of both the inner and outer worlds that few men ever reach.

Giraudoux, who was a great admirer of Nerval, wrote the following of him in a most perceptive essay:

The reading of *Aurélia* seems more moving to me because of the modesty with which Nerval confided his fate to his art, because of the confidence he had in his profession and the concern he had to prefer a literary form to a testament or a confidence. *Aurélia*, in my opinion, is a supreme lesson in poetry. The poet is he who reads his life, as one reads reversed writing in a mirror, and knows how to give it through that reflection that is talent and through literary truth, an order that it does not always have. Gérard de Nerval had been able to recognize that the elements of a poetic life had been distributed to him with abundance but without skillfulness . . . The woman who was to console him about another woman had come before the latter, not afterwards . . . The dreams which predicted sometimes followed the event . . . But there is no true poet who is not animated by a feeling of justice and pardon with respect to God, God who is perhaps unaware that men live in Time and that the events of their lives demand a sequence of causes and effects. In expanding, in shaping *Aurélia*, Nerval desired nothing more than to state life precisely as he had understood it. It is pleasant, —it is even the only pleasure for a writer —, to put his trust in his talent as in a personal and harmless demiurge. It is because talent, the joy of talent, has taken the upper hand over the other geniuses that straddled Nerval that *Aurélia*, far from presenting the incoherence and ambiguity of our present interpretations of dreams, gives the impression of a perfect logic, of a perfect beatitude, of a perfect consent . . . Just as each artisan becomes ennobled by dying the death that his profession calls for, our admiration for Nerval still grows in seeing that writer, at the extreme and diabolical point of his personal life, keep with it the proprieties and the joy of his profession.[1]

Although his purely literary output was not large, Nerval created a series of masterpieces in both poetry and prose that make him one of the glories of French literature. He was a gentle and dedicated artist who put the best of himself into his writings and thus survives as both man and artist, as human being and the creator of a brilliant literary world.

Notes and References

Chapter One

1. The standard edition of Nerval's works is his *Oeuvres,* edited by Albert Béguin and Jean Richer, published by Gallimard in *Bibliothèque de la Pléiade* (Paris, 1960–61), 2 vols. Although this edition is incomplete, it contains the majority of Nerval's important works in prose and poetry. References to Nerval's work in the present book, identified simply by volume and page numbers, are to this edition, except where otherwise noted. Because of the difficulty involved in translating Nerval's poetry, I have given the French texts in the notes so the reader may have available both the original and the translation. Owing to limitations of space, I have simply listed the volume and page numbers of the *Pléiade* edition in which can be found the original French of my prose translations. All translations from the French in this book are my own.

2. There is no good general study in English of French Romanticism. However, two books dealing with Romanticism in general are particularly valuable: Emery Neff, *A Revolution in European Poetry: 1660–1900* (New York, 1940), and Mario Praz, *The Romantic Agony* (Cleveland, 1967).

3. For a good study of the political background of the period see John B. Wolf, *France 1814–1919* (New York, 1963).

4. Pierre Moreau, *Le Romantisme* (Paris, 1962).

5. Quoted in Jean Giraud, *L'Ecole romantique française* (Paris, 1947), p. 8.

6. See Jean Richer, *Gérard de Nerval et les doctrines ésotériques* (Paris, 1947).

7. II, 402.

8. See Charles Dédéyan, *Gérard de Nerval et l'Allemagne* (Paris, 1959).

9. Gérard de Nerval, *La Vie des lettres,* ed. Jean Richer (Paris, 1959), p. 86.

10. I, 19.

11. Gérard de Nerval, *La Vie du théâtre,* ed. Jean Richer (Paris, 1961), p. 683.

Chapter Two

1. I, 20.

   Par mon amour et ma constance,
   J'avais cru fléchir ta rigueur
   Et le souffle de l'espérance
   Avait pénétré dans mon coeur;
   Mais le temps, qu'en vain je prolonge,
   M'a découvert la vérité,
   L'espérance a fui comme un songe . . .
   Et mon amour seul m'est resté!

2. I, 35.

   Du tronc à demi détachée
   Par le souffle des noirs autuns,
   Lorsque la branche désséchée
   Revoit les beaux jours du printemps,
   Si parfois un rayon mobile,
   Errant sur sa tête stérile,
   Vient brillanter ses rameaux nus,
   Elle sourit à la lumière;
   Mais la verdure printanière
   Sur son front ne renaîtra plus.

3. I, 34.

   . . . souvenir mouillé de pleurs
   Qui m'accable et répand son ombre
   Sur mes plaisirs et mes douleurs.

4. I, 23.

   Le papillon, fleur sans tige,
         Qui voltige,
   Que l'on cueille en un réseau;
   Dans la nature infinie,
         Harmonie
   Entre la plante et l'oiseau! . . .

5. I, 25.

   Une toute jeune fille
   Au coeur tendre, au doux souris,
   Perçant vos coeurs d'une aiguille,
   Vous contemple, l'oeil surpris

6. T. S. Eliot, *Collected Poems* (New York, 1936), p. 69.
   April is the cruellest month, breeding
   Lilacs out of the dead land, mixing
   Memory and desire, stirring
   Dull roots with spring rain.

7. I, 18.
> *Déjà les beaux jours, la poussière,*
> *Un ciel d'azur et de lumière,*
> *Les murs enflammés, les longs soirs;*
> *Et rien de vert: à peine encore*
> *Un reflet rougeâtre décore*
> *Les grands arbres aux rameaux noirs!*

8. *Ibid.*
> *Ce beau temps me pèse et m'ennuie.*

9. *Ibid.*
> *Le printemps verdissant et rose,*
> *Comme une nymphe fraîche éclose,*
> *Qui, souriante, sort de l'eau.*

10. In the latter part of the poem nature is seen as a possible temporary escape for the poet. In describing nature, the poet changes from the grating "i" sound of the first verse to more mellifluous vowels.

11. I, 23.
> *Quelque chose de vert*
> > *Avant l'hiver!*

12. I, 26.
> *. . . c'est que l'aigle seul—malheur à nous, malheur!*
> *Contemple impunément le Soleil et la Gloire.*

13. I, 36.
> *. . . à ma tristesse*
> *Que mon front pâle et sans jeunesse*
> *Ne doit plus sourire au bonheur?*

14. *Ibid.*
> *Mais à présent, ô jeune fille!*
> *Ton regard, c'est l'astre qui brille*
> *Aux yeux troublés des matelots,*
> *Dont la barque en proie au naufrage,*
> *A l'instant où cesse l'orage*
> *Se brise et s'enfuit sous les flots.*

15. I, 18.
> *Il est un air pour qui je donnerais*
> *Tout Rossini, tout Mozart et tout Weber,*

16. *Ibid.*
> *Qui pour moi seul a des charmes secrets!*

17. *Ibid.*
> *De deux cent ans mon âme rajeunit . . .*

18. I, 16.
> *C'est peut-être la seule au monde*
> *Dont le coeur au mien répondrait,*

Qui venant dans ma nuit profonde
D'un seul regard l'éclaircirait!
19. Ibid.
Elle a passé, la jeune fille.
20. Ibid.
Mais non, — ma jeunesse est finie . . .
Adieu, doux rayon qui m'as lui, —
Parfum, jeune fille, harmonie . . .
Le bonheur passait, — il a fui!
21. I, 15.
—rampante, avide et dégradée;
22. Ibid.
J'étais en poste, moi, venant de m'éveiller!
23. I, 17.
Notre-Dame est bien vieille: on la verra peut-être
Enterrer cependant Paris qu'elle a vu naître;
24. Ibid.
Mais, dans quelque mille ans, le Temps fera broncher
Comme un loup fait un boeuf, cette carcasse lourde,
Tordra ses nerfs de fer, et puis d'une dent sourde
Rongera tristement ses vieux os de rocher!
25. Ibid.
Bien des hommes, de tous les pays de la terre
Viendront, pour contempler cette ruine austère,
Rêveurs, et relisant le livre de Victor;
—Alors ils croiront voir la vieille basilique,
Toute ainsi qu'elle était, puissante et magnifique,
Se lever devant eux comme l'ombre d'un mort!
26. I, 19.
Moi seul j'y songe, et la pleure souvent;
Depuis trois ans, par le temps prenant force,
Ainsi qu'un nom gravé dans une écorce,
Son souvenir se creuse plus avant!
27. I, 17.
Il aime—et n'aime qu'une fois!
Qu'il est doux, paisible et fidèle,
Le nid de l'Oiseau—dans les bois!
28. Ibid.
Hélas! qu'elle doit être heureuse
La mort de l'Oiseau—dans les bois
29. I, 39.
A cette côte anglaise
J'ai donc fait mes adieux,

> *Et sa blanche falaise*
> *S'efface au bord des cieux.*

30. I, 40.

> *Joie, amour et délire,*
> *Hélas! trop expiés!*
> *Les rois sur le navire*
> *Et les dieux à leurs pieds!—*
>
> *Adieu, splendeur finie*
> *D'un siècle solennel!*
> *Mais toi seul, ô génie!*
> *Tu restes éternel.*

31. I, 1201.
32. I, 37.

> *Quand les feux du soleil inondent la nature,*
> *Quand tout brille à mes yeux et de vie et d'amour,*
> *Si je vois une fleur qui s'ouvre, fraîche et pure,*
>   *Aux rayons d'un beau jour;*
>
> *Si des troupeaux joyeux bondissent dans la plaine,*
> *Si l'oiseau chante aux bois où je vais m'égarer,*
> *Je suis triste et de deuil me sens l'âme si pleine*
>   *Que je voudrais pleurer.*

33. I, 38.

> *Mais quand je vois sécher l'herbe de la prairie,*
> *Quand la feuille des bois tombe jaune à mes pieds,*
> *Quand je vois un ciel pâle, une rose flétrie,*
>   *En rêvant je m'assieds.*
>
> *Et je me sens moins triste et ma main les ramasse,*
> *Ces feuilles, ces débris de verdure et de fleurs.*
> *J'aime à les regarder, ma bouche les embrasse . . .*
>   *Je leur dis: O mes soeurs!*

34. Ibid.

> *Ne vais-je pas aussi descendre dans la tombe,*
>   *Aux jours de mon printemps?*

35. Ibid.

> *Peut-être, ainsi que moi, cette fleur expirante,*
> *Aux ardeurs du soleil s'ouvrant avec transport,*
> *Enferma dans son sein la flamme dévorante*
>   *Qui lui donna la mort.*

36. Ibid.

> *Il le faut, ici-bas tout se flétrit, tout passe.*
> *Pourquoi craindre un destin que chacun doit subir?*

    La mort n'est qu'un sommeil. Puisque mon âme est lasse,
          Laissons-la s'endormir.

37. *Ibid.*
    Ma mère! . . . Oh! par pitié, puisqu'il faut que je meure,
    Amis, épargnez-lui des chagrins superflus,
    Bientôt elle viendra vers ma triste demeure,
          Mais je n'y serai plus.

38. *Ibid.*
    Et toi, rêve adoré de mon coeur solitaire,
    Belle et rieuse enfant que j'aimais sans espoir,
    Ton souvenir en vain me rattache à la terre;
          Je ne dois plus te voir.

    Mais si pendant longtemps, comme une image vaine,
    Mon ombre t'apparaît . . . oh! reste san effroi:
    Car mon ombre longtemps doit te suivre, incertaine
          Entre le ciel et toi.

39. I, 1200–1201.
    O mère des infortunés,
    Plaignez tous ceux qu'on abandonne:
    Soyez heureuse; et pardonnez
    Si vous voulez que Dieu pardonne.

40. I, 5.
    La connais-tu, Dafné, cette ancienne romance,
    Au pied du sycomore, ou sous les lauriers blancs,
    Sous l'olivier, le myrte, ou les saules tremblants,
    Cette chanson d'amour qui toujours recommence? . . .

41. *Ibid.*
    . . . le Temple au péristyle immense.

42. *Ibid.*
    Et les citrons amers où s'imprimaient tes dents,
    Et la grotte, fatale aux hôtes imprudents,
    Où du dragon vaincu dort l'antique semence? . . .

43. See Robert Graves, *The Greek Myths* (Baltimore, 1955), Vol. 1, pp. 194–99, for a more complete version of this myth.

44. Jean Richer, *Nerval: expérience et création* (Paris, 1970), p. 354.
    Connais-tu la contrée où dans le noir feuillage
    Brille comme un fruit d'or le fruit du citronnier,
    Où le vent d'un ciel bleu rafraîchit sans orage
    Les bocages de myrte et les bois de laurier?
    . . .

    Connais-tu la maison, le vaste péristyle
    Et la sombre caverne où dort le vieux serpent?

Richer claims that Nerval read the above in Toussenel's translation from the German, but Henri Lemaître, in his edition of Nerval, *Oeuvres* (Paris, 1958), Vol. 1, 700, claims that this is Nerval's translation.

45. I, 5.

> *Ils reviendront, ces Dieux que tu pleures toujours!*
> *Le temps va ramener l'ordre des anciens jours;*
> *La terre a tressailli d'un souffle prophétique . . .*

46. *Ibid.*

> *Cependant la sibylle au visage latin*
> *Est endormie encor sous l'arc de Constantin*
> *—Et rien n'a dérangé le sévère portique.*

47. I, 6.

> *. . . perdus dans le sommeil des bêtes.*

48. *Ibid.*

> *J'ai touché de mon front à la voûte éternelle;*
> *Je suis sanglant, brisé, souffrant pour bien des jours!*

49. *Ibid.*

> *Le dieu manque à l'autel où je suis la victime . . .*
> *Dieu n'est pas! Dieu n'est plus!*

50. I, 7.

> *"Immobile Destin, muette sentinelle,*
> *Froide Nécessité! . . . Hasard qui, t'avançant*
> *Parmi les mondes morts sous la neige éternelle,*
> *Refroidis, par degrés, l'univers pâlissant,*
>
> *"Sais-tu ce que tu fais, puissance originelle,*
> *De tes soleils éteints, l'un l'autre se froissant . . .*
> *Es-tu sûr de transmettre une haleine immortelle,*
> *Entre un monde qui meurt et l'autre renaissant? . . .*

51. *Ibid.*

> *Nul n'entendait gémir l'éternelle victime,*
> *Livrant au monde en vain tout son coeur épanché;*
> *Mais prêt à défaillir et sans force penché,*
> *Il appela le seul—éveillé dans Solyme:*
>
> *"Judas! lui cria-t-il, tu sais qu'on m'estime,*
> *Hâte-toi de me vendre, et finis ce marché:*
> *Je suis souffrant, ami! sur la terre couché . . .*
> *Viens! ô toi qui, du moins, as la force du crime!"*

52. I, 8.

Pilate is seen in a comparatively sympathetic way by Nerval, who says he had some pity for *ce fou*. Christ is, after all, the victim of God, not of Caesar or his emissary.

53. *Ibid.*

> *L'augure interrogeait le flanc de la victime,*
> *La terre s'enivrait de ce sang précieux . . .*
> *L'univers étourdi penchait sur ses essieux,*
> *Et l'Olympe un instant chancela vers l'abîme.*

> *"Réponds! criait César à Jupiter Ammon,*
> *Quel est ce nouveau dieu qu'on impose à la terre?*
> *Et si ce n'est un dieu, c'est au moins un démon . . ."*

> *Mais l'oracle invoqué pour jamais dut se taire;*
> *Un seul pouvait au monde expliquer ce mystère:*
> *—Celui qui donna l'âme aux enfants du limon.*

54. *Ibid.*

> *Eh quoi! tout est sensible!*

55. I, 8–9.

> *Homme! libre penseur—te crois-tu seul pensant*
> *Dans ce monde, où la vie éclate en toute chose:*
> *Des forces que tu tiens ta liberté dispose,*
> *Mais de tous tes conseils l'univers est absent.*

> *Respecte dans la bête un esprit agissant . . .*
> *Chaque fleur est une âme à la Nature éclose;*
> *Un mystère d'amour dans le métal repose:*
> *Tout est sensible; —Et tout sur ton être est puissant!*

> *Crains dans le mur aveugle un regard qui t'épie:*
> *A la matière même un verbe est attaché . . .*
> *Ne la fais pas servir à quelque usage impie.*

> *Souvent dans l'être obscur habite un Dieu caché;*
> *Et, comme un oeil naissant couvert par ses paupières,*
> *Un pur esprit s'accroît sous l'écorce des pierres.*

56. I, 42.

> *. . . un esprit des cieux sur la terre exilé.*

57. I, 41.

> *Pourquoi mit-il encor ce pénible fardeau*
> *Sur ma tête aux pensers tristes abandonnée,*
> *Et souffrante, et déjà de soi-même inclinée?*

58. *Ibid.*

> *Oh! ces feux du couchant vermeils, capricieux,*
> *Montent comme un chemin splendide, vers les cieux!*
> *Il semble que Dieu dise à mon âme souffrante:*
> *Quitte le monde impur, la foule indifférente,*

Suis d'un pas assuré *cette route qui luit,*
Et—viens à moy, mon fils . . . et—n'attends pas LA NUIT! ! !

59. I, 26.
Où sont nos amoureuses?
Elles sont au tombeau:
Elles sont plus heureuses,
Dans un séjour plus beau!

60. I, 43.
Madame et souveraine,
Que mon coeur a de peine . . .

The same song, known as "Voi che sapete," is sung by Cherubino in
Mozart's *Le Nozze di Figaro.*

61. *Ibid.*
Je suis un fainéant, bohème journaliste,
Qui dîne d'un bon mot étalé sur son pain.
Vieux avant l'âge et plein de rancunes amères,
Méfiant comme un rat, trompé par trop de gens,
Ne croyant nullement aux amitiés sincères. . . .

62. I, 44.
Sans feu dans mon taudis, sans carreaux aux fenêtres,

63. *Ibid.*
. . . le joint *du ciel ou de l'enfer,*
Et j'ai pour l'autre monde enfin bouclé mes guêtres.

64. *Ibid.*
J'ai fait mon épitaphe et prends la liberté
De vous la dédier dans un sonnet stupide
Qui s'élance à l'instant du fond d'un cerveau vide . . .
Mouvement de coucou par le froid arrêté:
La misère a rendu ma pensée invalide!

65. *Ibid.*
Il a vécu tantôt gai comme un sansonnet,
Tour à tour amoureux insoucieux et tendre,
Tantôt sombre et rêveur comme un triste Clitandre,
Un jour il entendit qu'à sa porte on sonnait.

C'était la Mort! Alors il la pria d'attendre
Qu'il eût posé le point à son dernier sonnet;
Et puis sans s'émouvoir, il s'en alla s'étendre
Au fond du coffre froid où son corps frissonait.

Il était paresseux, à ce que dit l'histoire,
Il laissait trop sécher l'encre dans l'écritoire.
Il voulait tout savoir mais il n'a rien connu.

> *Et quand vint le moment où, las de cette vie,*
> *Un soir d'hiver, enfin l'âme lui fut ravie,*
> *Il s'en alla disant: "Pourquoi suis-je venu?"*

66. Gérard de Nerval, *La Vie des lettres,* (Vol. 1 of *Oeuvres complémentaires de Gérard de Nerval*) edited by Jean Richer, (Paris, 1959), p. 89.

67. I, 158–59.

68. I, 3.

The text of the complete sonnet follows:

> *Je suis le Ténébreux,—le Veuf,—l'Inconsolé,*
> *Le Prince d'Aquitaine à la Tour abolie:*
> *Ma seule* Étoile *est morte, —et mon luth constellé*
> *Porte le* Soleil noir *de la* Mélancolie.
>
> *Dans la nuit du Tombeau, Toi qui m'as consolé,*
> *Rends-moi le Pausilippe et la mer d'Italie,*
> *La* fleur *qui plaisait tant à mon coeur désolé,*
> *Et la treille où le Pampre à la Rose s'allie.*
>
> *Suis-je Amour ou Phoebus?... Lusignan ou Biron?*
> *Mon front est rouge encor du baiser de la Reine;*
> *J'ai rêvé dans la Grotte où nage la Sirène...*
>
> *Et j'ai deux fois vainqueur traversé l'Achéron:*
> *Modulant tour à tour sur la lyre d'Orphée*
> *Les soupirs de la Sainte et les cris de la Fée.*

69. Carlyle A. Pushong, *The Tarot of the Magi* (London, 1967), p. 69.

70. I, 3.

> *Car la Muse m'a fait l'un des fils de la Grèce.*

71. This realm of fire is also the land of the Cainites which Adoniram visits in *Voyage en Orient.*

72. I, 3.

> *Je sais pourquoi là-bas le volcan s'est rouvert...*
> *C'est qu'hier tu l'avais touché d'un pied agile,*
> *Et de cendres soudain l'horizon s'est couvert.*

73. I, 4.

> *Depuis qu'on duc normand brisa tes dieux d'argile,*
> *Toujours, sous les rameaux du laurier de Virgile,*
> *Le pâle hortensia s'unit au myrte vert!*

74. *Ibid.*

> *Le dieu Kneph en tremblant ébranlait l'univers:*
> *Isis, la mère, alors se leva sur sa couche,*

Fit un geste de haine à son époux farouche,
Et l'ardeur d'autrefois brilla dans ses yeux verts.

"Le voyez-vous, dit-elle, il meurt, ce vieux pervers,
Tous les frimas du monde ont passé par sa bouche,
Attachez son pied tors, éteignez son oeil louche,
C'est le dieu des volcans et le roi des hivers!

"L'aigle a déjà passé, l'esprit nouveau m'appelle,
J'ai revêtu pour lui la robe de Cybèle...
C'est l'enfant bien-aimé d'Hermès et d'Osiris!"

La déesse avait fui sur sa conque dorée,
La mer nous renvoyait son image adorée,
Et les cieux rayonnaient sous l'écharpe d'Iris.

75. I, 13.
L'aigle a déjà passé: Napoléon m'appelle;...

76. I, 4–5.
Tu demandes pourquoi j'ai tant de rage au coeur
Et sur un col flexible une tête indomptée;
C'est que je suis issu de la race d'Antée,
Je retourne les dards contre le dieu vainqueur.

Oui, je suis de ceux-là qu'inspire le Vengeur,
Il m'a marqué le front de sa lèvre irritée,
Sous la pâleur d'Abel, hélas! ensanglantée,
J'ai parfois de Caïn l'implacable rougeur!

Jéhovah! le dernier, vaincu par ton génie,
Qui, du fond des enfers, criait: "O tyrannie!"
C'est mon aïeul Bélus ou mon père Dagon...

Ils m'ont plongé trois fois dans les eaux du Cocyte,
Et, protégeant tout seul ma mère Amalécyte,
Je ressème à ses pieds les dents du vieux dragon.

77. There is a distinction, however, in Nerval's mind between the children of the earth—those descended from Adam, and the children of fire—those descended from Cain.

78. I, 5–6. The text of the complete sonnet follows:
La Treizième revient... C'est encor la première;
Et c'est toujours la Seule,—ou c'est le seul moment:
Car es-tu Reine, ô Toi! la première ou dernière?
Es-tu Roi, toi le seul ou le dernier amant?...

Aimez qui vous aima du berceau dans la bière;
Celle que j'aimai seul m'aime encor tendrement:
C'est la Mort—ou la Morte . . . O délice! ô tourment!
La rose qu'elle tient, c'est la Rose trémière.

Sainte napolitaine aux mains pleines de feux,
Rose au coeur violet, fleur de sainte Gudule:
As-tu trouvé ta Croix dans le désert des cieux?

Roses blanches, tombez! vous insultez nos Dieux,
Tombez, fantômes blancs, de votre ciel qui brûle:
—La Sainte de l'abîme est plus sainte à mes yeux!

79. Nerval's obsession with the word *seul* (alone) when it is a question of love (I alone loved; she alone loves me, etc.) is found in many of his works. It indicates the special, personal, and private meaning that love has for him, and it takes on, in his writings, certain mystic connotations.

80. Gérard de Nerval, *Oeuvres*, ed. Henri Lemaître, *op. cit.*, p. 703.

Chapter Three

1. II, 14.

2. II, 19.

3. For a list and discussion of sources of *Voyage en Orient*, the reader should peruse the introduction of Henri Lemaître to his edition of the work: Gérard de Nerval, *Oeuvres, op. cit.*, Vol. II, v-xi.

4. I, 150.

5. II, 361.

6. II, 362.

7. Incest is a major theme of many Romantic writers. It is found most often in the works of Chateaubriand and Byron, but it is also found in Shelley and Poe. Later it becomes a theme of Flaubert and Swinburne. For further reading on the subject, see Mario Praz, *The Romantic Agony* (Cleveland, 1967), pp. 109–10.

8. II, 363.

9. II, 365.

10. II, 380–81.

11. II, 389–90.

12. This opera, which is available on a private label, follows rather closely the story told by Nerval. The only major omissions are the use of the bird Hud-Hud and the descent to the city of Enochia.

13. II, 553.

14. II, 529–30.

15. II, 509.

16. II, 552.
17. II, 564.
18. I, 79–80.
19. I, 82.
20. I, 89.
21. I, 102.
22. I, 104.
23. I, 107–8.
24. I, 109.
25. *Ibid.*
26. I, 118.
27. Arsène Houssaye was the editor of *L'Artiste*. At one time Houssaye (1815–96) was Director of the Théâtre Français, and his fascinating *Confessions: souvenirs d'un demi-siècle (1830–1880)* cast much light on the period about which Nerval writes in the *Petits Châteaux de Bohème*, specifically the period of the early eighteen thirties.
28. See Chapter 2.
29. I, 65.
30. I, 66.
31. I, 70–71.
32. I, 75.
33. I, 73.
34. I, 75.
35. See Chapter 2.
36. Richer, *Nerval, expérience et création, op. cit.*, p. 294.
37. I, 220.
38. Nerval, *Oeuvres*, ed. Henri Lemaître, *op. cit.*, p. 506. "Amendement dirigé *'contre tout écrit ayant la forme d'un roman et passible d'un droit de timbre supplémentaire.'* "
39. I, 189.
40. I, 192.
41. I, 208.
42. I, 177.
43. I, 189.
44. I, 194.
45. I, 239.
46. I, 363.
47. I, 241.
48. *Ibid.*
49. I, 242.
50. I, 243.
51. I, 244.

52. *Ibid.*
53. *Ibid.*
54. I, 246.
55. *Ibid.*
56. I, 246–47.
57. I, 255.
58. Cf. *El Desdichado*, line 14. Sylvie, unlike Adrienne who was a saint, is identified by Nerval as a fairy.
59. I, 256.
60. I, 257.
61. I, 262.
62. I, 266.
63. I, 271.
64. I, 272.
65. I, 287–88.
66. I, 288.
67. Cf. line 10 of *Artémis*, I, 5.
68. Again the "fairy" makes an appearance. The fairy takes part in the magic aspects of life, while the saint is part of the mystical aspects.
69. I, 289.
70. I, 290.
71. Cf. line 14 of *El Desdichado*, I, 3. "Les soupirs de la Sainte et les cris de la Fée."
72. I, 292.
73. The trip of which Nerval speaks took place in 1834 rather than 1832. Other sections or details are memories of his trip to Italy in 1843. This blending of time periods puts *Octavie* in the realm of fiction, but fiction based on certain real incidents.
74. *Isis* is based on a work by Carl A. Böttiger, *Die Isis-Vesper*.
75. I, 294.
76. I, 296.
77. I, 297.
78. I, 299–300.
79. I, 300.
80. I, 301.
81. *Ibid.*
82. *Ibid.*
83. I, 301–2.
84. I, 302.
85. I, 303.
86. *Ibid.*
87. I, 304.

88. I, 306–7.
89. I, 308.
90. I, 320.
91. I, 356.
92. I, 347.
93. *La Vita nuova* is Dante's first work. It demonstrates the poet's growth to spiritual and artistic maturity. Nerval's *Aurélia*, which is also autobiographical in character, shows a similar progression.
94. Cf. Charles Mauron, *Des Métaphores obsédantes au mythe personnel* (Paris, 1963), pp. 64–80.
95. I, 359.
96. *Ibid.*
97. I, 361.
98. This is perhaps a reference to the star of Melancholia that Nerval had seen in Durer's etching. This star appears frequently, and always with ominous connotations, in Nerval's works.
99. Nerval is undoubtedly thinking of Paul, the writer of the *Epistles* because his friend is the namesake of the Saint.
100. I, 363.
101. Cf. *Fantaisie*, I, 18–19.
102. I, 364.
103. *Composition en abyme* is a term that is used especially to describe Gide's fictional technique in *Les Faux-Monnayeurs*. Gide, the novelist, is writing a novel about a novelist writing a novel. Gide, at the same time, is keeping a diary about his thoughts about the work, as Edouard, the main character in Gide's novel, is keeping one about his. Thus there are many levels and points of view in the work.
104. I, 365.
105. Actually this is a reminiscence of his uncle's house in Morte-fontaine.
106. I, 367.
107. *Ibid.*
108. I, 368.
109. Nerval often seems to feel that, despite his knowledge of the occult and his abilities of psychic perception, he is often coming close to secrets that man has no right to know. The mystic universe in Nerval is delicately balanced, and, in *Aurélia* especially, the poet is afraid of upsetting the balance by penetrating too far into its mysteries.
110. I, 374.
111. *Ibid.*
112. Cf. *La Grand'mère*, I, 19. Passage of time in Nerval intensifies the poet's sense of loss of his loved ones.

113. Jean Richer, in his edition of *Aurélia*–Gérard de Nerval, *Aurélia* (Paris, 1965), p. 37, writes, "Two visitors to the clinic at Montmartre, A. Esquiros and an anonymous person, said that they had seen around 1842 the sketches of Nerval on a wall."
Cf. Richer, *Nerval: expérience et création, op. cit.*, pp. 438–40.
114. I, 375.
115. I, 368. Nerval wrote a footnote to this passage which is of interest. "Seven was the number of Noah's family, but one of the seven was mysteriously connected with the previous generations of the Elohim! . . .
"Like a bolt of lightning, my imagination showed me the multiple gods of India as images of the family that was so to speak primatively concentrated. I shudder to go further for a fearful mystery still lies in the Trinity . . . We were born under biblical law . . ." I, 368–69.
116. I, 376.
117. Richer, *Nerval: expérience et création, op. cit.*, p. 478.
118. I, 381.
119. *Ibid.*
120. I, 382.
121. I, 384.
122. I, 385.
123. *Ibid.*
124. *Ibid.*
125. *Ibid.*
126. I, 385–86.
127. I, 386.
128. I, 387.
129. I, 388.
130. I, 391.
131. Note again the use of the word "alone."
132. I, 393.
133. I, 394.
134. I, 396.
135. I, 399.
136. I, 400. Nerval became more and more impressed by Napoleon as he grew older, and it is not therefore surprising that in his states of madness he identified with the French Emperor who, in Nerval's mind, had attained a state of semidivinity.
137. I, 403.
138. I, 404.
139. *Ibid.*
140. Richer says in a footnote, I, 1272: "One may suppose, if it is a question of a work note, that the letters are 'sent' to Jenny Colon,

or else that he had directed a text of letters to be inserted in *Aurélia* to Ulbach. But what text? Gautier and Houssaye filled the space left in the *Revue de Paris* of February 15, 1855 with a version of the letters to Jenny Colon. Nothing proves that it is the text announced by Gérard. It is better to leave the lacuna."

141. I, 407.
142. I, 408.
143. I, 412.
144. I, 413.
145. I, 413–14.
146. Nerval, *La Vie des lettres, op. cit.*, p. 20.
147. *Ibid.*, p. 6.
148. *Ibid.*, p. 19.

Chapter Four

1. Nerval, *La Vie des lettres*, edited by J. Richer (Paris, 1959), p. xii. All the essays discussed in this chapter are to be found in this volume and in Nerval, *La Vie du théâtre*, ed. Richer (Paris, 1961) which form Volumes 1 & 2 of the *Oeuvres complémentaires de Gérard de Nerval*.
2. *Ibid.*, p. 238.
3. *La Vie du théâtre*, p. 519.
4. *La Vie des lettres*, p. 112.
5. *Ibid.*, p. 114.
6. *La Vie du théâtre*, p. 611.
7. *La Vie des lettres*, p. 108.
8. *La Vie du théâtre*, p. 682.
9. *La Vie des lettres*, pp. 137–38.
10. *Ibid.*, pp. 139–40.
11. *Ibid.*, pp. 140–41.
12. *La Vie du théâtre*, p. 701.
13. *Ibid.*, p. 615.
14. *Ibid.*, p. 558.
15. *Oeuvres*, I, 1138.
16. Cf. *La Vie du théâtre*, pp. 570, 590, 683.

Chapter Five

1. Jean Giraudoux, *Littérature* (Paris, 1944), pp. 100–101.

Selected Bibliography

The following list is, of necessity, a summary one designed for the general reader. Its aim is to present some useful editions of Nerval's works, bibliographies of writings by and about Nerval, and some important studies of his work.

PRIMARY SOURCES

1. Editions

There is no complete edition of Nerval's works. The three best approximations are:

GÉRARD DE NERVAL, *Oeuvres complètes.* Ed. Aristide Marie, Jules Marsan, and Edouard Champion. Paris: Champion, 1926–32, 6 vols.
—————, *Oeuvres.* Ed. Albert Béguin and Jean Richer. Paris: Gallimard, 1960–61, 2 vols.
—————, *Oeuvres.* Ed. Henri Lemaître. Paris: Garnier, 1958, 2 vols.

2. Individual Editions

A series of volumes entitled *Oeuvres complémentaires de Gérard de Nerval,* edited by Jean Richer (Paris: Minard) has been appearing since 1959. The following volumes have already been published:

   I. *La Vie des lettres* (1959)
  II. *La Vie du théâtre* (1961)
 III. *Théâtre* (1965)
  V. *Théâtre* (1967)
 VI. *Le Prince des sots* (1960)
VIII. *Variétés et fantaisies* (1964)

Other individual editions that are valuable are the following:

GÉRARD DE NERVAL, *Voyage en Orient.* Ed. Gilbert Rouger. Paris: Richelieu, 1950, 4 vols.
—————, *Les Chimères.* Ed. Jeanine Moulin. Geneva: Droz, 1949.
—————, *Les Chimères.* Ed. Jean Guillaume. Brussels: Palais des Académies, 1966.

181

—————, *Pandora.* Ed. Jean Guillaume. Gembloux: Duculot, 1968.
—————, *Aurélia.* Ed. Jean Richer. Paris: Minard, 1965.
—————, *Sylvie. Aurélia.* Ed. Raymond Jean. Paris: Corti, 1964.
—————, *Les Filles du feu. Les Chimères.* Ed. L. Cellier. Paris:
   Garnier-Flammarion, 1965.

3. Translations

GÉRARD DE NERVAL, *Selected Writings.* Tr. G. Wagner. Ann Arbor:
   Univ. of Michigan Press, 1957. This volume contains translations
   of *Sylvie, Emilie, Aurélia,* and selections from the poetry.
—————, *Daughters of Fire—Sylvie, Emilie, Octavie.* Tr. James
   Whitall. New York: N. L. Brown, 1922.
—————, *The Women of Cairo.* Tr. Conrad Elphinstone. London: G.
   Routledge & Sons, 1929.

SECONDARY SOURCES

1. Bibliographies

The most nearly complete bibliography of writings by and about
Nerval may be compiled from the following sources:

THIEME, *Bibliographie de la littérature française de 1800 à 1930.*
   Paris: Droz, 1933; and from its continuations; under the same
   title and by the same publisher:
DREHER and ROLLI, 1930–39.
DREVET and THIEME, 1940–49.

Publications from 1950 to the present can be found in the quarterly
bibliographies of *La Revue d'histoire littéraire de la France* (RHLF)
and *La Revue de littérature comparée* (RCL) as well as in the annual
bibliographies of PMLA.

Four excellent bibliographies devoted exclusively to Nerval are:

LÉON CELLIER, *Où en sont les recherches sur Gérard de Nerval?*
   Paris: Minard, 1957.
JEAN SENLIER, *Gérard de Nerval. Essai de bibliographie.* Paris:
   Nizet, 1959.
—————, *Bibliographie nervalienne (1960–1967).* Paris: Nizet, 1968.
JAMES VILLAS, "Present State of Nerval Studies: 1957 to 1967,"
   French Review xli, no. 2 (1967), 221–31.

2. Books

BÉGUIN, ALBERT, *Gérard de Nerval*. Paris: Corti, 1945. Excellent introduction to Nerval and his works.

CATTAUI, GEORGES, *Orphisme et prophétie chez les poètes français 1850–1950*. Paris: Plon, 1965. Contains an illuminating, if not very original, chapter on Nerval.

CELLIER, LÉON, *Gérard de Nerval, l'homme et l'oeuvre*. Paris: Boivin, 1956. One of the better "life and works" books. It contains many fine insights into the mind and works of Nerval.

DÉDÉYAN, CHARLES, *Gérard de Nerval et l'Allemagne*. Paris: Société d'édition d'enseignement supérieur, 1957–1959. 3 vols. The best analysis of the influence of Germany on Nerval's thought and art.

DURRY, MARIE-JEANNE, *Gérard de Nerval et le mythe*. Paris: Flammarion, 1956. A first-rate analysis of the role of myth in Nerval's works.

HAEDENS, KLÉBER, *Gérard de Nerval ou la sagesse romantique*. Paris: Grasset, 1939. Extremely short, very superficial, somewhat impressionistic essay on Nerval.

MARIE, ARISTIDE, *Gérard de Nerval, le poète, l'homme*. Paris: Hachette, 1914, reprinted 1950. The best of the early studies of Nerval. Still informative and useful.

MOREAU, PIERRE, *Sylvie et ses soeurs nervaliennes*. Paris: Société d'enseignement supérieur, 1966. A sensitive study of Nerval's heroines and the role of memory and dream in his work.

POULET, GEORGES, *Les Métamorphoses du cercle*. Paris: Plon, 1961. Contains a fine essay on Nerval's imaginative process. One of the better essays by the New Critics on Nerval.

RICHARD, JEAN-PIERRE, *Poésie et profondeur*. Paris: Ed. du Seuil, 1955. Another New Critic looks at Nerval. A good essay but less incisive than Poulet's.

RHODES, S. A., *Gérard de Nerval: Poet, Traveller, Dreamer*. New York: Philosophical Library, 1951. The only book I have found on Nerval in English. This study is more a slightly romanticized, but well-written biography than a critical study of his works.

RICHER, JEAN, *Gérard de Nerval et les doctrines ésotériques*. Paris: Ed. du Griffon d'or, 1947. What the title says it is. A well-documented study.

—————, *Nerval: expérience et création*. Paris: Hachette, 1970. The single best book on Nerval. A brilliant study of the process of artistic creation.

Index

185